AN INTRODUCTION TO
LIQUID HELIUM

BY

J. WILKS

CLARENDON PRESS · OXFORD

1970

Oxford University Press, Ely House, London W. 1

GLASGOW   NEW YORK   TORONTO   MELBOURNE   WELLINGTON
CAPE TOWN   SALISBURY   IBADAN   NAIROBI   DAR ES SALAAM   LUSAKA   ADDIS ABABA
BOMBAY   CALCUTTA   MADRAS   KARACHI   LAHORE   DACCA
KUALA LUMPUR   SINGAPORE   HONG KONG   TOKYO

PRINTED IN NORTHERN IRELAND
BY THE UNIVERSITIES PRESS
BELFAST

OXFORD LIBRARY OF
THE PHYSICAL SCIENCES

Editors

B. BLEANEY   D. H. WILKINSON
J. EISINGER

OXFORD LIBRARY OF
THE PHYSICAL SCIENCES

Already published

THE SPECTRUM OF ATOMIC HYDROGEN
By G. W. SERIES

ELECTROMAGNETIC STRUCTURE OF NUCLEONS
By S. D. DRELL and F. ZACHARIASEN

NUCLEAR SIZES
By L. R. B. ELTON

NOISE IN ELECTRICAL CIRCUITS
By F. N. H. ROBINSON

THE THIRD LAW OF THERMODYNAMICS
By J. WILKS

THE TWO-NUCLEON INTERACTION
By M. J. MORAVCSIK

THEORIES OF NUCLEAR FISSION
By L. WILETS

COULOMB EXCITATION
By L. C. BIEDENHARN & P. J. BRUSSARD

HIGH ENERGY REACTIONS
By A. B. CLEGG

THEORY OF DIRECT NUCLEAR REACTIONS
By W. TOBOCMAN

THE FUNDAMENTAL ATOMIC CONSTANTS
By J. H. SANDERS

ANGULAR MOMENTUM
SECOND EDITION
By D. M. BRINK & G. R. SATCHLER

PREFACE

LIQUID ^{4}He exhibits many unusual effects, and is unique in that under certain conditions it flows through a fine capillary with apparently a complete absence of viscosity and friction. Moreover, liquid ^{3}He and ^{4}He, although chemically similar, have quite different physical properties, ^{3}He being governed by Fermi statistics and ^{4}He by Bose statistics. In fact, the properties of liquid helium present the most striking example of the influence of quantum statistics, and the symmetry of the wave function, on the macroscopic behaviour of a physical system. This volume has therefore been designed as an abridged form of my larger book *The Properties of Liquid and Solid Helium*, to present a more general account of the properties of liquid ^{3}He and ^{4}He.

I have tried to provide an overall view of the wide variety of characteristic properties of liquid helium, while at the same time going into sufficient details of basic points to show that there is now a sound theoretical basis underlying the experimental results. The task of producing a book of moderate size has imposed some difficult tasks of selection. It has been necessary to cut some corners, to omit much experimental detail, and to abbreviate some of the theoretical arguments. However, the reader who wishes for more information on almost any of the topics mentioned will find them treated at greater length in my longer book. Similarly, the references given here refer only to a few leading papers, to the sources of the diagrams, and to some recent work. For a complete bibliography the reader is again referred to the longer book.

Finally, I wish to thank Dr. H. M. Rosenberg who read the manuscript and made helpful comments. I am indebted to the authors and publishers who have allowed me to reproduce their diagrams; the source of all these figures is indicated in the captions. It is also a pleasure to thank the officers of the Clarendon Press for their continued helpful advice and assistance.

Clarendon Laboratory, Oxford   J. WILKS
October 1969

CONTENTS

CHAPTER I

INTRODUCTION

LIQUID helium exists in two isotopic forms, liquid ^{3}He and liquid ^{4}He. The most important characteristic of both liquids is that under their saturated vapour pressures they remain liquid down to the very lowest temperatures. We begin by indicating how this comes about.

1.1. The permanent liquids

The helium atom is spherically symmetrical, and smaller than that of any other element. The only binding forces in the liquid are Van der Waals forces, which arise from the fluctuating polarization charges induced in the electron shells of adjacent atoms. These forces are weaker than in all other substances, so the critical and boiling points of helium (Table 1.1) are the lowest of all.

In nearly all substances, the freezing point is determined by a balance between the Van der Waals forces and the thermal energy. The attractive forces tend to pack the molecules into a regular crystalline lattice, while the thermal energy tends to disrupt an ordered arrangement. However, in liquid helium both the attractive forces and the thermal energy are extremely small. It thus comes about that another contribution to the balance of forces, usually negligible, must be taken into account. This is the effect of the so-called zero-point energy.

To a first approximation, we may regard an atom in the solid as a harmonic oscillator, and its ground-state energy is given by the Schrödinger equation as $\frac{1}{2}h\nu_0$, where ν_0 is the characteristic frequency and h is Planck's constant. Alternatively, we may picture an atom in the liquid as a free particle located in a small cage formed by the adjacent atoms; the

TABLE 1.1

The critical temperature T_C, and normal
boiling point T_B, of liquid ^{3}He and ^{4}He

	^{3}He	^{4}He
$T_C(K)$	3·32	5·20
$T_B(K)$	3·19	4·21$_5$

energy of the lowest state is then $h^2/8mV^{2/3}$, where m is the mass of the atom, and V the volume of the cage. In both cases the energy is lowered if the molar volume increases, hence the effect of this ground-state, or zero-point, energy is to increase the molar volume.

Fig. 1.1 shows the potential energy of both liquid and solid ^{4}He as a function of molar volume, calculated from the known force fields of the helium atoms and their spatial arrangement

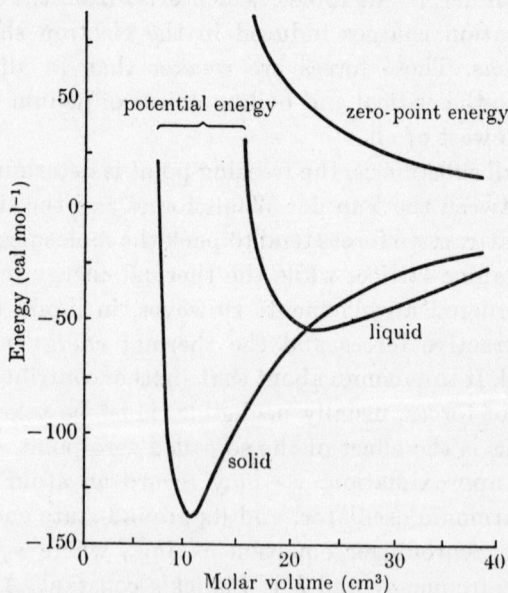

FIG. 1.1. Estimated values of the potential and zero-point energy of liquid and solid ^{4}He at absolute zero, as functions of the molar volume (London [1]).

in the liquid and solid, as shown by X-ray scattering measurements. In a normal liquid the stable state at absolute zero would be that with the lowest internal energy. In this case we would expect the solid to be stable with a molar volume of about 10 cm³, but when considering condensed helium we must include the effect of zero-point energy. The figure shows an estimate given by F. London for this zero-point energy, which he assumed to be approximately the same in both the solid and liquid phases.

At absolute zero the total energy of the liquid is just the sum of the potential and zero-point energies, and we see from Fig. 1.1 that it is least for a molar volume of about 30 cm³. This estimate is in good agreement with the observed molar volume of the liquid of 28 cm³. As the zero-point energy is inversely proportional to the mass of the atom, its effect is relatively greater in liquid ^{3}He, which has a molar volume of about 40 cm³ even though the atoms are the same size as those of ^{4}He.

Fig. 1.1 also implies that at a molar volume of about 30 cm³, liquid ^{4}He has a lower energy than the solid, and is therefore the stable form. In fact, more detailed calculations are necessary to establish this point unambiguously. The difference between the potential energies of the solid and liquid phases is small, so we are not justified in using the same value of the zero-point energy for each phase. Although a full calculation becomes quite involved, there is no doubt that helium remains liquid because the zero-point energy leads to a large molar volume.

Finally we note that both liquid ^{3}He and ^{4}He are colourless, they have densities of about 0·07 and 0·14 g cm^{-3} respectively; and liquid ^{3}He has a much higher vapour pressure as the atoms are less tightly bound.

1.2. The melting curve

Liquid helium may be solidified by the application of pressure. The stable state of a system is that with the lowest free energy, defined in terms of the usual thermodynamic

variables as

$$G = U - TS + PV.$$

At absolute zero, under the saturated vapour pressure, this condition reduces to the internal energy U being a minimum. However, if we apply pressure to the liquid and solid, the PV term contributing to the free energy is different for the two

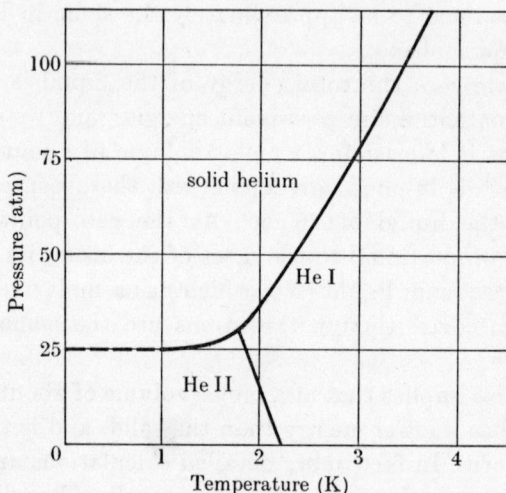

FIG. 1.2. The melting pressure and lambda line of liquid ^{4}He (Swenson [2]).

phases. The solid then becomes the stable phase at higher pressures.

The pressure required to solidify liquid ^{4}He is shown in Fig. 1.2. Below 1 K, this melting pressure becomes virtually independent of temperature, and the gradient of the melting curve decreases approximately as T^8. (We ignore for the moment an extremely small variation in the melting pressure which we discuss in section 4.4.) According to the Clausius-Clapeyron equation

$$\left(\frac{dP}{dT}\right)_m = \frac{\Delta S_m}{\Delta V_m},$$

where ΔS_m and ΔV_m are the entropy and volume changes on melting. Measurements of the volume change show that ΔV_m

takes up a finite and constant value at low temperatures. Hence the entropy difference ΔS_m tends to zero, a result which is in accord with the Third Law of Thermodynamics. The entropies of both the solid and liquid vary approximately as T^3, therefore the entropy difference ΔS_m varying as T^8 falls off much more rapidly. Hence over an appreciable range of temperature, there is almost no heat of melting, and liquid and solid along the melting curve have virtually the same entropy. As we normally think of a liquid as a more disordered phase than a solid, it is not surprising that the liquid exhibits unusual properties.

1.3. Liquid ³He and liquid ⁴He

At first sight, liquid ³He and liquid ⁴He are not very different from the other inert gas liquids, except for their large molar volume. In fact, using the simple kinetic theory of gases we can account, with moderate success, for the thermal and kinetic properties of the liquids near to their boiling points. However, at lower temperatures, both liquids show very marked deviations from this quasi-classical behaviour.

In liquid ⁴He the change in behaviour is marked by a very characteristic anomaly in the specific heat, the so-called lambda transition (Fig. 1.3). The specific heat rises to a very high value at the lambda temperature of 2·17 K, and then falls off rapidly. Immediately below this transition temperature the liquid becomes *superfluid*, that is, it can flow through very fine channels with apparently no viscosity at all! In addition it exhibits a whole range of other unique properties.

The properties of liquid ³He above 1 K are quite similar to those of liquid ⁴He near the boiling point, as we might expect since the two atoms have electron shells which are almost identical. Yet at lower temperatures all resemblance ceases. Liquid ³He shows no lambda transition, and is not superfluid. However, below 1 K its properties show a gradual change to a new scheme of behaviour quite different from that of a normal liquid. We now go on to describe both liquids in detail. We

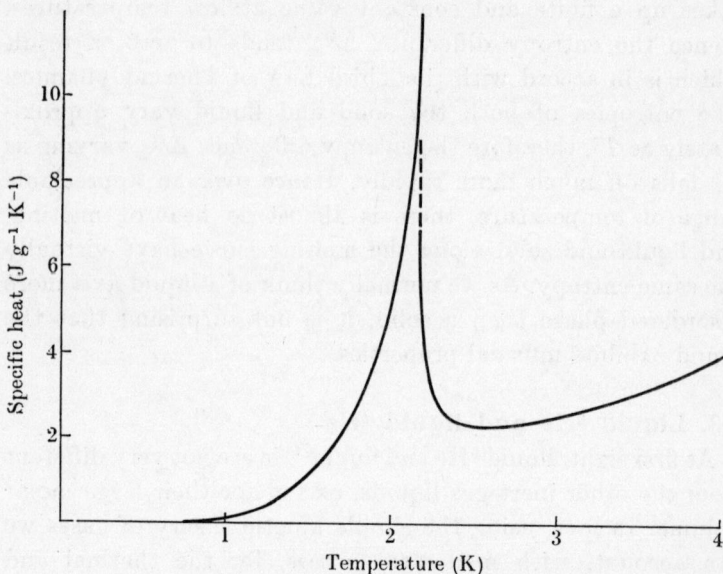

FIG. 1.3. The specific heat of liquid ^{4}He under the saturated vapour pressure (after Atkins [3]).

shall see that the differences between liquid helium and other liquids, and between ^{3}He and ^{4}He, come about because liquid ^{3}He is governed by Fermi statistics, and liquid ^{4}He by Bose statistics. We begin by considering liquid ^{3}He.

CHAPTER II

LIQUID ^{3}He

ABOVE 1 K, liquid ^{3}He behaves somewhat like a dense classical gas, but at lower temperatures there is a transition to a quite different regime. We now outline some of the main features of this region.

2.1. The specific heat and susceptibility

Although we do not intend to give detailed descriptions of experimental arrangements, two features of work with liquid ³He are particularly noteworthy. The transition to the low temperature region only becomes complete at temperatures below 0·05 K, and measurements down to at least a few

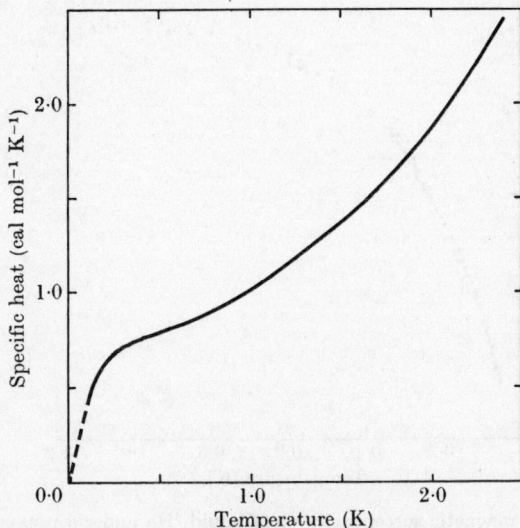

FIG. 2.1. The specific heat of liquid ³He under the saturated vapour pressure (after references [5–7]).

millikelvins are necessary for a full study of the liquid. These are much lower temperatures than are found necessary in work on ⁴He, and call for specialized techniques, both to attain the temperatures and to achieve thermal equilibrium within the experiment (see for example reference [4]). In addition the supply of ³He was initially very restricted, and even today experiments are usually designed to use no more than 1 or 2 cm³ of liquid.

The specific heat has been measured by a number of workers, as shown in Fig. 2.1. At the lowest temperatures, it appears to be varying almost, but not quite, linearly with temperature. The measurements below 0·05 K may be fitted to a curve of

the form

$$C/R = \alpha T - \beta T^2,$$

where R is the gas constant, T the absolute temperature, and α and β positive constants. We can thus estimate that the specific heat has a limiting value, as T tends to zero, of about $2\cdot9\,RT$ (measured at $0\cdot12$ atm). This value, it should be

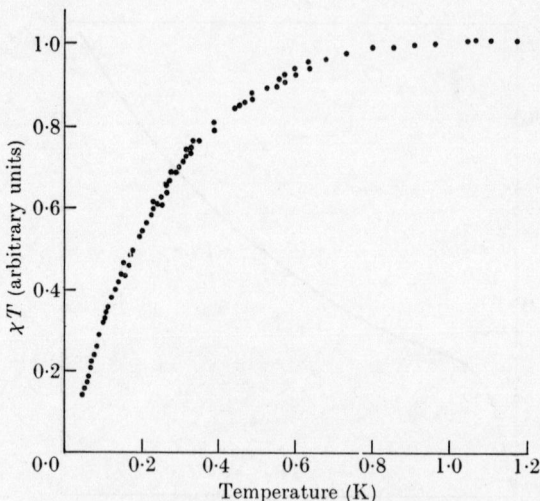

FIG. 2.2. The magnetic susceptibility χ of liquid ^{3}He under a pressure of $0\cdot5$ atm, as a function of the temperature.   The product χT is plotted against T in arbitrary units (after Thomson, Meyer, and Adams [8]).

noted, is appreciably different from that given by the mean slope between zero and $0\cdot1$ K.

Fig. 2.2 shows the magnetic susceptibility χ arising from the nuclear spin of $\frac{1}{2}$ associated with each ^{3}He atom, plotted in the form of χT versus T. At high temperatures the susceptibility varies as $1/T$ (i.e. χT is constant), but as the temperature is reduced the susceptibility falls below this value, and finally becomes independent of temperature (i.e. χT is proportional to T).

2.2. The transport coefficients

Above 1 K the coefficient of viscosity is approximately independent of temperature, but it begins to increase rapidly

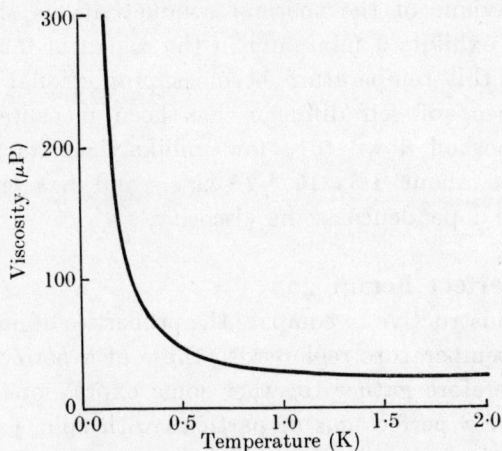

FIG. 2.3. The viscosity of liquid ³He (after Betts, Osborne, Welber, and Wilks [9], and Betts, Keen, and Wilks [10]).

below 0·5 K (Fig. 2.3). The viscosity at lower temperatures has been deduced from observations of the absorption of sound waves, and by observing the damping on an oscillating crystal. Although the results from these different methods are not in too good agreement, the viscosity appears to have a value of the order of $3/T^2$ micropoise.

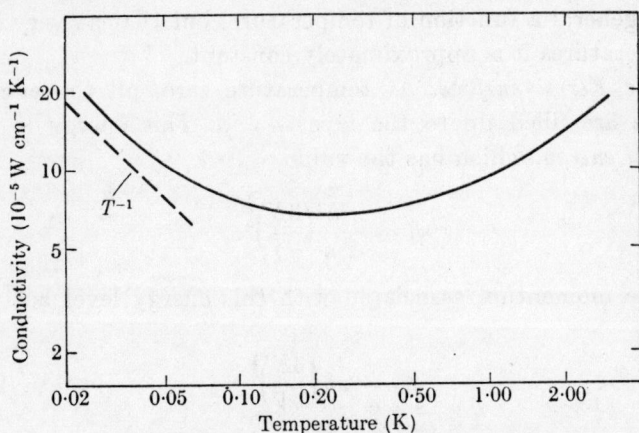

FIG. 2.4. The thermal conductivity of liquid ³He (after Lee and Fairbank [11], and Anderson, Salinger, and Wheatley [12]).

The behaviour of the thermal conductivity is shown in Fig. 2.4. It exhibits a minimum in the region of 0·2 K, and then below this temperature becomes proportional to $1/T$. The coefficient of self diffusion has been measured by a magnetic method down to a few millikelvins. Its value is found to be about $1·5 \times 10^{-6}/T^2$ c.g.s., and has the same temperature dependence as the viscosity.

2.3. The perfect Fermi gas

It is now instructive to compare the properties of liquid ³He in the low temperature region with those of a perfect Fermi gas. We therefore gather together some expressions for the properties of a perfect gas of particles with spin $\frac{1}{2}$ obeying Fermi statistics in the degenerate low temperature region. We consider an assembly of N atoms of mass m in a volume V.

The distribution function giving the number of atoms with energy ϵ is given by the usual methods of statistical mechanics for an assembly of identical Fermi particles as

$$n(\epsilon) = \{e^{(\epsilon-\mu)/k_\mathrm{B}T}+1\}^{-1},$$

where k_B is Boltzmann's constant, and μ the chemical potential specified by the condition $\sum_\epsilon n(\epsilon) = N$. Note that μ is in general a function of temperature, but that at very low temperatures it is approximately constant.

The Fermi surface. At temperature zero, all the energy levels are filled up to the level $\epsilon = \mu$. This energy is the *Fermi energy*, which has the value

$$\mu = \frac{\pi^2\hbar^2}{2m}\left(\frac{3N}{\pi V}\right)^{\frac{2}{3}}.$$

The momentum associated with this energy level has the value

$$p_0 = \pi\hbar\left(\frac{3N}{\pi V}\right)^{\frac{1}{3}}. \tag{2.1}$$

The boundary of the filled levels (at temperature zero) in momentum space is termed the *Fermi surface*, and for an isotropic system takes the form of the surface of a sphere of radius p_0. In a *degenerate* Fermi gas (i.e. $k_B T \ll \mu$) the distribution function $n(\epsilon)$ does not differ greatly from its value at absolute zero. In fact $n(\epsilon)$ only differs from its zero-temperature value over a small range of energy, of order $k_B T$, close to the Fermi surface (see Fig. 2.5).

Another important parameter is the so-called *density of states*, that is the number of levels per unit energy range. The

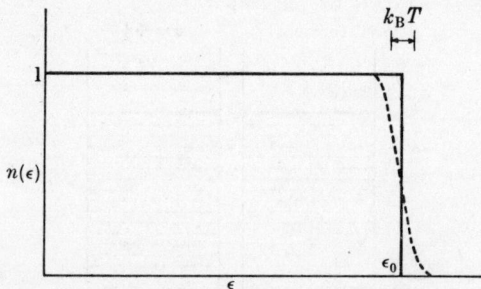

FIG. 2.5. Schematic diagram of the Fermi-Dirac distribution function. The full line shows the distribution for $T = 0$; the dotted line corresponds to a somewhat higher temperature T.

density of states is proportional to the volume of the gas, but it is often convenient to work with a parameter which depends only on the density. In addition, for a degenerate Fermi system, it is generally sufficient to consider only the value of this parameter at the Fermi surface. We therefore introduce the quantity $(d\tau/d\epsilon)$, the density of states for unit volume of gas, which has the value at the Fermi surface of

$$\left(\frac{d\tau}{d\epsilon}\right)_0 = \frac{m}{\pi\hbar^2}\left(\frac{3N}{\pi V}\right)^{\frac{1}{3}} = \frac{m}{\pi^2\hbar^3}\,p_0. \qquad (2.2)$$

The specific heat per unit volume is obtained by differentiating the internal energy of the whole system, and is found to have the value

$$\mathscr{C} = \tfrac{1}{3}\pi^2 k_B^2 \left(\frac{d\tau}{d\epsilon}\right)_0 T. \qquad (2.3)$$

We shall also find it useful to quote a result for the velocity of

sound c, viz

$$c^2 = \frac{p_0^2}{3m^2}.$$

The magnetic susceptibility. In the presence of a magnetic field H, the energy of a level includes an additional term $-2\beta\sigma H$, where β is the nuclear magnetic moment, and σ the spin coordinate is either $\pm\frac{1}{2}$. Thus the effect of applying a magnetic field is to shift all the levels with spin $\frac{1}{2}$ relative to

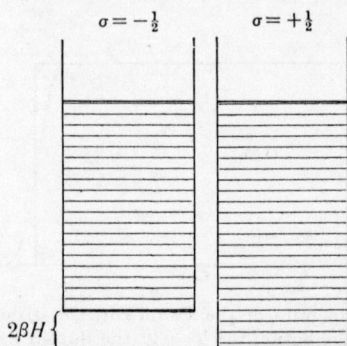

FIG. 2.6. Schematic diagram of the relative displacement of the energy levels with spin $\frac{1}{2}$ in the presence of a magnetic field; see text.

those with spin $-\frac{1}{2}$ by an amount $-2\beta H$. In equilibrium there is an excess number of atoms, Δ per unit volume, with spins parallel to the field (see Fig. 2.6), where

$$\Delta = 2\beta H \left\{ \frac{1}{2} \left(\frac{d\tau}{d\epsilon} \right)_0 \right\}.$$

Hence there is a net magnetic moment $\beta\Delta$, and the susceptibility per unit volume is

$$\chi = \frac{\beta\Delta}{H} = \beta^2 \left(\frac{d\tau}{d\epsilon} \right)_0,$$

which is independent of the temperature.

2.4. Liquid ³He as a Fermi gas

Both liquid ³He and a degenerate Fermi gas have a specific heat varying linearly with temperature, and a nuclear susceptibility which is independent of temperature. We now compare the numerical values of the specific heat C, the velocity of sound c, and the volume susceptibility χ of liquid ³He under the saturated vapour pressure, with those for a perfect gas of the same density. The results of this comparison in the low-temperature region are shown in Table 2.1. We see that the properties of the liquid are of the same order of magnitude as those of the perfect gas, but that they differ by an appreciable factor.

TABLE 2.1

	Observed	Perfect gas	Ratio
$C(\text{J mol}^{-1}\text{ K}^{-1})$	$2 \cdot 9\ RT$	$1 \cdot 00_3\ RT$	$2 \cdot 9$
$c(\text{m s}^{-1})$	183	95	$1 \cdot 92$
$\chi(\text{c.g.s.})$	$3 \cdot 3 \times 10^{38}\ \beta^2$	$3 \cdot 61 \times 10^{37}\ \beta^2$	$9 \cdot 1$

(R is the gas constant, and β the magnetic moment of the ³He nucleus.)

The parallel between the behaviour of liquid ³He and a Fermi gas is much strengthened when we consider transport coefficients such as the viscosity. According to the elementary kinetic theory of gases, the viscosity may be written

$$\eta = \tfrac{1}{3}\rho\tau v^2,$$

where τ (do not confuse with $d\tau$) is the mean time between collisions, and v the mean velocity of the atoms. We can show quite simply, for a gas obeying the Fermi statistics, that τ varies rapidly with temperature. When a collision occurs, two particles with energies ϵ_1 and ϵ_2 scatter into two different levels with energies ϵ_3 and ϵ_4 (such that $\epsilon_1 + \epsilon_2 = \epsilon_3 + \epsilon_4$). According to the Fermi statistics, this process is only possible if the levels ϵ_3 and ϵ_4 are unoccupied before the collision. Now, the form of the distribution function is such that the only empty levels accessible to the scattering atoms are those in the range $\Delta\epsilon \simeq k_B T$ shown in Fig. 2.5. Therefore the probability of finding two empty levels is proportional to $(\Delta\epsilon)^2$, that is to $(k_B T)^2$. Hence we conclude that

$$\tau \propto 1/T^2.$$

Moreover, as the only atoms able to scatter are those close to the Fermi surface, their velocity will approximate to the value v_0 at the surface, and be independent of T. Hence we conclude that

$$\eta \propto \tau \propto 1/T^2.$$

The coefficients of *thermal conductivity* and *self diffusion*, K and D, are given by simple kinetic theory as

$$K = \tfrac{1}{3}\rho\tau v^2 C \quad \text{and} \quad D = \tfrac{1}{3}\tau v^2,$$

where C is the specific heat. Hence, by similar arguments to those used for the viscosity, we deduce that

$$K \propto 1/T, \qquad D \propto 1/T^2.$$

We cannot calculate the absolute values of these coefficients without knowing the collision cross-sections of the atoms, but it is clear that the predicted dependences on temperature are similar to those observed in liquid ^{3}He. We conclude that the properties of the liquid are controlled to a large extent by the Fermi statistics. Thus a Fermi gas model of liquid ^{3}He gives a fair representation of its properties, but is by no means exact or complete.

CHAPTER III

THE LANDAU THEORY OF A FERMI LIQUID

WE now outline Landau's theory of a Fermi liquid, which commences with a gas-like model, and then takes account of the interactions between the atoms (Landau [13]).

3.1. The Landau model

The essence of Landau's model is illustrated schematically in Fig. 3.1. The left-hand side of the diagram shows the energy levels of a degenerate perfect gas governed by the Fermi

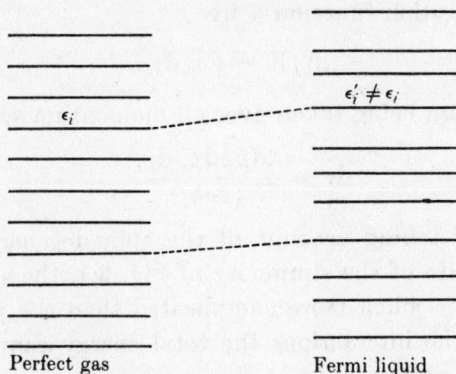

FIG. 3.1. Schematic diagram of the energy levels of a perfect gas and a Fermi liquid. Corresponding levels have the same wave number but different energies; see text.

statistics. The energies of the levels are uniquely determined by the properties of the individual atoms, and are calculated by solving the Schrödinger equation for one atom occupying the total volume. As the gas is assumed to be degenerate, the distribution function only varies in the region of the Fermi surface, as in Fig. 2.5. The momentum of an atom on the Fermi surface is, as previously noted,

$$p_0 = \pi\hbar\left(\frac{3N}{\pi V}\right)^{\frac{1}{3}}. \tag{3.1}$$

Landau next uses a perturbation method to introduce the interactions between the atoms. He assumes that these interactions can be gradually turned on, thus modifying the energy of each level. He also assumes that the wave number, or momentum, of each level is unchanged. In particular the momentum of a particle on the Fermi surface is still given by (3.1). When the full interaction has been introduced, each level has (in general) a different energy, as is indicated schematically on the right-hand side of Fig. 3.1. We now consider the properties of this new system.

The number of particles N in a volume V is given in terms of the distribution function n by

$$N/V = \int n \, d\tau, \tag{3.2}$$

the integration being taken over all momentum space so that

$$d\tau = \frac{2 dp_x \, dp_y \, dp_z}{(2\pi\hbar)^3},$$

the factor 2 taking account of the spin degeneracy of the levels. In spite of the simplicity of Fig. 3.1, the system with interactions is much more complicated than the perfect gas. Because of the interactions the total energy cannot now be written as a simple sum

$$U/V = \sum_i n_i \epsilon_i,$$

where the n_i and ϵ_i are the occupation number and energy of the ith level. The energy of a level ϵ_i is no longer a unique function for an atom, but depends on the occupation numbers of all the levels. It is in fact no longer clear what we mean by the 'energy of an atom'. Landau therefore *defines* an energy ε by the relation

$$\delta U/V = \int \epsilon \, \delta n \, d\tau, \tag{3.3}$$

where δU is the change in energy of the whole system when a small change δn is made in the distribution function. (In general this energy will depend on the nuclear spin, but for many purposes we can regard ^{3}He as an isotropic liquid, and then symmetry requirements imply that the energies do not depend on the spin parameter.)

The energy ϵ defined by equation (3.3) is the energy of an atom interacting with all the other N particles *with a particular distribution*. Before turning on the interactions, the energy of the atom was related to its momentum and wave number by the usual energy spectrum

$$\epsilon = p^2/2m = \hbar^2 k^2/2m.$$

On introducing interactions, this simple relation characteristic of a real free particle is no longer valid, so we say that equation (3.3) defines the energy of a *quasi-particle*. That is, we replace the system of real particles by a system of quasi-particles, which describe the atomic motion in a way which (as we show below) is tractable to calculation.

3.2. The distribution function and energy spectrum

We now find an expression for the number $n(\epsilon)\, d\epsilon$ of quasi-particles with energies in the range ϵ to $\epsilon + d\epsilon$. This distribution is found in the normal way by maximizing the entropy, subject to keeping the total energy and the total number of quasi-particles (equal to the number of atoms) constant. Hence

$$n(\epsilon) = \{e^{(\epsilon - \mu)/k_B T} + 1\}^{-1}, \qquad (3.4)$$

where μ, the chemical potential, is determined by the condition.

$$N/V = \int n\, d\tau.$$

At first sight it appears that the distribution function we have obtained is just the Fermi function for a perfect gas. However, relation (3.4) is much more complex, because ϵ is now a function of n, and the general form of this expression is rather unmanageable. However, the Landau theory is only concerned with the behaviour of the liquid at the lowest temperatures. In this case the distribution approximates to the usual Fermi step function, so it is approximately constant, and we may discuss the distribution in terms of its departure from the Fermi surface at temperature zero.

One effect of introducing the interactions is that (in general) the wave functions of the various levels will no longer be true eigenfunctions, and transitions will occur between the different levels. These transitions introduce an uncertainty $\delta\epsilon$ into the energy of a state, in accord with the uncertainty principle

$$\delta\epsilon \sim \hbar/\tau,$$

where τ is the lifetime of a state. This uncertainty places a restriction on the validity of the model. As the distribution function approximates to a Fermi function, the properties of the system are determined (like those of the gas) by the distribution of those quasi-particles lying in the energy range $\Delta\epsilon \sim k_B T$ close to the Fermi surface (Fig. 2.5). Clearly a discussion in terms of these energy levels is only meaningful if

$$\delta\epsilon < \Delta\epsilon. \tag{3.5}$$

It turns out that τ, which is equal to the time between collisions of the quasi-particles, varies as $1/T^2$ as for a perfect gas. Hence $\delta\epsilon$ is proportional to T^2, whereas $\Delta\epsilon$ is proportional to T. Therefore condition (3.5) can always be satisfied at a sufficiently low temperature.

We can now write down an expression for the energy spectrum, or dispersion relation, $\epsilon(p)$ of the quasi-particles near the Fermi surface. These particles lie in an energy range of order $k_B T \ll \mu$, so that at sufficiently low temperatures $\epsilon \simeq \mu$. It is then a good approximation to write

$$\epsilon = \mu + \left(\frac{\partial\epsilon}{\partial p}\right)_0 (p - p_0), \tag{3.6}$$

where $(\partial\epsilon/\partial p)_0$ is evaluated at the Fermi surface. In the case of a perfect gas

$$\left(\frac{\partial\epsilon}{\partial p}\right)_0 = \frac{p_0}{m} = v_0,$$

where v_0 is the velocity of a particle at the Fermi surface. In the Landau theory $(\partial\epsilon/\partial p)_0$ has a different value, but by analogy we write

$$\left(\frac{\partial\epsilon}{\partial p}\right)_0 = \frac{p_0}{m^*} = v_0,$$

where m^* and v_0 are two new parameters. m^* is known as the effective mass, and the energy spectrum (3.6) now takes the form

$$\epsilon = \mu + \frac{p_0}{m^*}(p - p_0). \tag{3.7}$$

According to Landau, the energy ϵ may be regarded as the Hamiltonian of a quasi-particle. In this case the relation $(\partial\epsilon/\partial p)_0 = v_0$ is the quantum version of Hamilton's equation

$\partial H/\partial p = \dot{q}$, and v_0 is therefore taken to be the velocity of a quasi-particle on the Fermi surface.

Another important parameter is the density of states at the Fermi surface. This function is determined by the form of the energy spectrum at the Fermi surface, and its value is obtained by replacing m by m^* in the corresponding expression for a perfect gas, i.e.

$$\left(\frac{\mathrm{d}\tau}{\mathrm{d}\epsilon}\right)_0 = \frac{m^*}{\pi\hbar^2}\left(\frac{3N}{\pi V}\right)^{\frac{1}{3}}. \tag{3.8}$$

3.3. The interaction function

The energy ϵ of a level in the isotropic liquid is specified by the relation

$$\delta U/V = \int \epsilon \, \delta n \, \mathrm{d}\tau. \tag{3.3}$$

That is, the energy of a quasi-particle is the first functional derivative of the total energy with respect to the distribution function. We also require an expression for the change in energy of a particular level due to a redistribution of particles in the other levels. This is

$$\epsilon(\mathbf{p}) = \epsilon_0(\mathbf{p}) + \int f(\mathbf{p}, \mathbf{p}') \, \delta n' \, \mathrm{d}\tau',$$

where

$$f(\mathbf{p}, \mathbf{p}') = \frac{\partial^2 U}{\partial n(\mathbf{p}) \, \partial n'(\mathbf{p}')}.$$

In this relation $\epsilon_0(\mathbf{p})$ is the energy of the level with momentum $\mathbf{p}$, in an equilibrium distribution at temperature $T = 0$. The quantity $\epsilon(\mathbf{p})$ is the energy of the same level (with momentum $\mathbf{p}$) when the occupation of the other levels ($\mathbf{p}'$) differs from the zero-temperature distribution by an amount $\delta n'(\mathbf{p}')$. Thus the function $f(\mathbf{p}, \mathbf{p}')$ specifies how the energy of a level is modified by the occupation of the other levels. As we will be concerned only with particles close to the Fermi surface, $p \simeq p' \simeq p_0$; hence in the first approximation $f(\mathbf{p}, \mathbf{p}')$ is a function only of χ, the angle between $\mathbf{p}$ and $\mathbf{p}'$. That is,

$$f(\mathbf{p}, \mathbf{p}') = f(\chi).$$

In order to express the interaction function in its most convenient form, Landau introduces a new function F defined as

$$F(\chi) = \left(\frac{d\tau}{d\epsilon}\right)_0 f(\chi), \tag{3.9}$$

where $(d\tau/d\epsilon)_0$ is the density of states given by (3.8). He then expands $F(\chi)$ in Legendre polynomials so that

$$F = \sum_n F_n P_n(\cos \chi) = F_0 + F_1 \cos \chi + F_2\left(\frac{3 \cos^2\chi - 1}{2}\right) + \ldots,$$

where the F_n are constants to be determined. This expansion is important because a comparison of theory with experiment suggests that the principal contributions to F come from the leading terms. Hence we are able to specify the complex interactions in the liquid by only the first two or three of the constants F_n, as we show in the next section.

To discuss the behaviour of liquid ³He in a magnetic field, it is necessary to introduce the spin coordinate σ. We will not discuss this in detail, but note that Landau rewrites (3.3) as

$$\delta U/V = \tfrac{1}{2}\mathrm{Sp}_\sigma \int \epsilon \, \delta n \, d\tau. \tag{3.10}$$

The terms ϵ and n are now matrices, and the symbol Sp_σ implies the summing of the diagonal elements of the matrix product within the integral. The factor $\tfrac{1}{2}$ appears because we have already taken account of the two spin states in our definition of $d\tau$. Similarly we must rewrite equation (3.2) as

$$N/V = \tfrac{1}{2}\mathrm{Sp}_\sigma \int n \, d\tau. \tag{3.11}$$

The spin coordinate affects the total energy of the system through its effect on the exchange energy, which is the additional term in the expression for the electrostatic interaction between the atoms which arises when we use symmetrical wave functions to describe a system of identical particles. The total wave function of liquid ³He must be antisymmetric because it obeys Fermi statistics. Hence, if we turn over one spin and thus change the symmetry of the spin wave function, the symmetry of the spatial wave function must also change so that the total wave function remains antisymmetric. This change in the spatial function will alter the value of the exchange integral; hence the total energy is a function of the spin coordinates. Therefore it comes about that the state of lowest energy is generally one where the nuclear spins take up either a parallel or antiparallel alignment.

To introduce the exchange force into the Landau model, the interaction function $f(\chi)$ is extended to include a term depending on the spin coordinates $\boldsymbol{\sigma}$, $\boldsymbol{\sigma}'$, viz.

$$\mathscr{F}(\mathbf{p}, \boldsymbol{\sigma}; \mathbf{p}', \boldsymbol{\sigma}') = f(\mathbf{p}, \mathbf{p}') + \zeta(\mathbf{p}, \mathbf{p}')\boldsymbol{\sigma} \cdot \boldsymbol{\sigma}'.$$

We also introduce a function $G(\chi)$, analogous to $F(\chi)$ in equation (3.9), so that

$$G(\chi) = \left(\frac{\mathrm{d}\tau}{\mathrm{d}\epsilon}\right)_0 \zeta(\chi) = G_0 + G_1 \cos \chi + \cdots$$

We are now able to specify the exchange interaction quite well by the values of the constants G_0 and G_1 in the two leading terms.

3.4. The properties of liquid ³He

We now relate the Landau model to the properties of the liquid. Straightforward calculations show that at sufficiently low temperatures the temperature dependences of the specific heat, susceptibility, and transport coefficients are the same as those of the perfect gas. However the absolute magnitudes are all different, being related in a rather complicated way to the parameters of the theory. The constants F_0, F_1, and G_0 are specified exactly by the relations

$$C = \frac{m^*}{m}C_g \qquad \frac{m^*}{m} = (1 + \tfrac{1}{3}F_1) \qquad (3.12)$$

$$c^2 = \frac{p_0^2}{3m^2}\frac{1 + F_0}{1 + \tfrac{1}{3}F_1}. \qquad (3.13)$$

$$\chi = \frac{m^*}{m}(1 + \tfrac{1}{4}G_0)^{-1}\chi_g, \qquad (3.14)$$

where C_g and χ_g are the specific heat and susceptibility of a perfect gas of the same density. Values for these constants derived from the measured specific heat, velocity of sound, and susceptibility are given in Table 3.1.

The specific heat of the liquid is greater than that of the gas (equation (2.3)) because the interactions increase the density of states at the Fermi surfaces in the ratio m^*/m, and the specific heat is proportional to this quantity. So far as the susceptibility is concerned the effect of the interactions shows itself in two ways. Like the specific heat, it depends directly

TABLE 3.1

Fermi liquid parameters for liquid ^{3}He

Specific heat	$2{\cdot}9\,RT$ J mol^{-1} K^{-1}		
Velocity of sound	$183{\cdot}4$ m s^{-1}		
m^*/m 2·9		F_0 9·6	
G_0 −2·7		F_1 5·6	

on the density of levels at the Fermi surface, and is therefore augmented by a factor m^*/m. There is also an additional effect arising from the spin-dependent exchange forces, which give rise to the term $(1+\tfrac{1}{4}G_0)^{-1}$. Experimentally it is found that the susceptibility of liquid ^{3}He in the Fermi region is much higher than that of a perfect gas of the same density, so the constant G_0 is negative. Hence the exchange forces favour parallel alignment of the spins, in contrast to the Fermi statistics which tend to produce anti-parallel alignment. This effect is quite large, as the term $\tfrac{1}{4}G$ turns out to have a value of about −0·7. Indeed the form of (3.14) implies that if the exchange forces were about 50 per cent stronger ($\tfrac{1}{4}G_0 < -1$), the ground state of the liquid would be ferromagnetic.

The Landau theory also predicts the magnitude of the transport coefficients by setting up and solving a Boltzmann transport equation for the motion of the quasi-particles in steady but non-uniform conditions. The temperature dependence of the coefficients of viscosity η, thermal conductivity K, and self diffusion D, turn out to be similar to those of the perfect gas, in accord with the measured values. The absolute values of the transport coefficients are obtained after somewhat lengthy calculations, in terms of the parameters F_n and G_n. Substituting in the known values of F_0, F_1, and G_0 (which also suffice to define G_1), values are obtained for the coefficients of conductivity and diffusion which are in reasonable agreement with the measured values under pressures of 0·28 and 27 atm, particularly in view of the neglect of F_2, G_2, and higher terms. The theory also gives a fair account of the magnitude and pressure dependence of the viscosity, although the experimental values deduced from different methods vary considerably. For some recent refinements of these calculations see references [14] and [15].

We conclude that the Landau theory gives quite a satisfactory account of the properties of liquid ^{3}He. In particular it shows that the temperature dependence of the specific heat, susceptibility, and transport coefficients is a direct consequence of the Fermi distribution function. Thus liquid ^{3}He provides the most direct and striking example of the effect of the Fermi statistics.

3.5. Zero sound

We have now shown that the Landau theory gives a comprehensive account of the specific heat, velocity of sound, susceptibility, and transport properties. However, as F_0, F_1, and G_0 are used as independent adjustable parameters, we have not made too vigorous a verification of the theory. A crucial feature of the Landau theory is that it predicts the existence, at sufficiently low temperatures, of an entirely new mode of sound propagation, the so-called zero sound (Landau [16]).

We have already mentioned that the relaxation time characterizing the collisions between the quasi-particles varies as $1/T^2$. Hence, at sufficiently low temperatures, the time between collisions becomes greater than the period of any sound wave. At first sight it would appear that the propagation of sound is then impossible. The position would be partly analogous to attempting to propagate a sound wave in a rarefied gas with a mean free path greater than the wavelength of the sound. In fact a perfect Fermi gas cannot support a wave motion at very low temperatures. However, liquid ^{3}He does not behave as a perfect gas, because of the strong interactions between the atoms.

Landau's treatment of the propagation of sound of angular frequency ω starts from the Boltzmann equation for the distribution function of the quasi-particles, and derives the response of the distribution function to a periodic disturbance. In the limit $\omega\tau \ll 1$ the disturbance is ordinary hydrodynamical sound. However, other wave solutions can be obtained if $\omega\tau \gg 1$, the possibility of observing these solutions depending on the strength of the interactions. Landau names these new wave modes 'zero sound'. The theory predicts modes of zero sound analogous to ordinary sound, viscous waves, and spin waves, but virtually all experiment and discussion has centred on the mode similar to ordinary sound.

It turns out that two characteristics of the zero-sound mode are a different velocity and a different coefficient of absorption from those of ordinary sound. In general, the velocity will depend on the values of all the constants F_n; however, if we use the only values we know (F_0 and F_1), we find that the velocity in the zero-sound region should be greater by about 6 m s^{-1}. The absorption in the ordinary region arises principally from the viscosity and may be written as

$$\alpha = A\omega^2\eta,$$

where A is a constant, and η, the viscosity, varies as $1/T^2$. The behaviour in the zero-sound region is quite different, viz.

$$\alpha_0 = A_0 T^2,$$

where A_0 is a constant which is independent of the frequency.

To observe zero sound it is necessary to use very high frequency sound waves or rather low temperatures, so the experiments are not too straightforward. Hence, the new mode was first detected by measuring the reflection coefficient of a sound wave in a quartz crystal, when incident on a face in contact with the liquid. The value of this reflection coefficient leads directly to the acoustic impedance of the liquid, Z, which

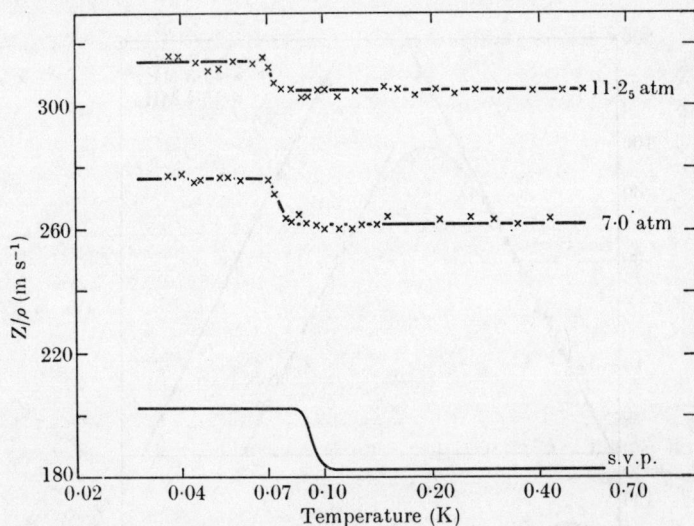

FIG. 3.2. The acoustic impedance of liquid ^{3}He, expressed as the ratio Z/ρ, as a function of pressure (Betts, Keen, and Wilks [10]).

for an ordinary liquid has the value

$$Z = \rho c,$$

where ρ is the density, and c the velocity of sound. An analysis of the situation in the zero-sound region shows that the impedance $Z_0 \simeq \rho c_0$ where c_0 is the velocity of zero sound. Hence measurements of the acoustic impedance indicate the transition to zero sound (Fig. 3.2).

From measurements of the viscosity we can estimate values of the relaxation time, and hence show that at the transition temperature $\omega\tau \sim 1$, as we would expect. The shift in the transition temperature with increasing pressure correlates with the change in τ as deduced from values of the viscosity as a function of pressure. Also, the change in the value of Z/ρ is of the calculated order of magnitude, and decreases with increasing pressure, as we expect from the values of F_0 and F_1 appropriate to the liquid at higher densities.

Fig. 3.3 shows subsequent measurements of the velocity and absorption. The transition again occurs at the expected

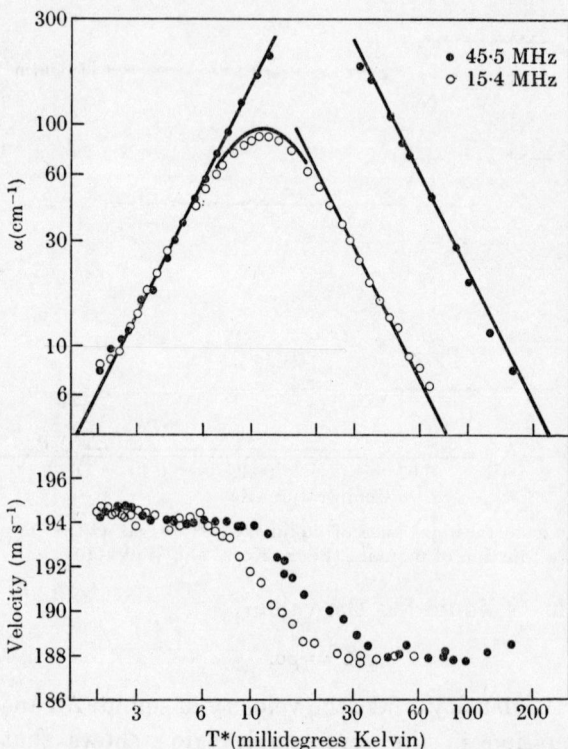

FIG. 3.3. The amplitude attenuation coefficient α and the velocity of sound and zero sound in liquid ³He (Abel, Anderson and Wheatley [17]).

temperature, and the change in velocity is 6 m s⁻¹, the value we calculate by ignoring F_1 and higher terms. Note in particular that the low temperature absorption has the expected dependence on frequency and temperature. We conclude that all the features of zero sound as predicted by the theory are essentially correct. However various points of interest remain. In particular the theory leads us to expect that

Z_0/ρ should be equal to or less than c_0, whereas we find $Z_0/\rho > c_0$; this point is further discussed in reference [18].

CHAPTER IV

MISCELLANEOUS ASPECTS OF LIQUID ³He

WE now touch briefly on some other features of liquid ³He which are of particular interest.

4.1. The atomic theory of liquid ³He

The Landau theory gives quite a good account of the properties of liquid ³He, yet it has to make the basic assumption that the thermal motion of the liquid can be described by elementary excitations, or quasi-particles, of the type proposed. There remains a considerable problem in theoretical physics. The force fields of helium atoms are tolerably well known. The excitation model of the liquid given by Landau is well corroborated by the experimental evidence. There remains the task of providing a rigorous demonstration by quantum mechanics that an assembly of such atoms really does behave as an assembly of quasi-particles. There is a very extensive literature on these topics and we shall only indicate the main lines of discussion.

The theoretical problem is to solve the Schrödinger equation for an assembly of ³He atoms with an appropriate force field. There is little difficulty in writing down the appropriate Hamiltonian, but the resulting equation is so complicated that it appears hopeless to obtain an exact solution. One of the usual methods of dealing with this type of problem is to use perturbation techniques. That is we begin with a Hamiltonian H_0 of a simpler system for which we can obtain exact solutions, and which differs from the real Hamiltonian H by a term H' which is relatively small. We then write

$$H = H_0 + \lambda H',$$

where λ may take values between 0 and 1, and assume that we can obtain solutions and eigenvalues in the form

$$\psi = \psi_0 + \lambda\psi_1 + \lambda^2\psi_2 + \dots$$
$$W = W_0 + \lambda W_1 + \lambda^2 W_2 + \dots$$

This procedure implies that the behaviour of the actual system can be attained from that of the simpler system by a gradual and steady increase in the value of the parameter λ, and we return to this point in the next section.

Several authors have given perturbation treatments of liquid ³He, starting with a perfect gas as the initial simple system, and then introducing an interaction potential. It has thus been established that the thermal motion of the atoms in the liquid may be described in terms of quasi-particles with Landau's energy spectrum. Moreover, as assumed by Landau, the wave number of a quasi-particle at the Fermi surface is the same as for an atom in the perfect gas, while the density of the levels is enhanced by the interactions. These authors also show that the exchange part of the interaction energy leads to a preference for parallel alignment of the nuclear spins, which opposes the preference for anti-parallel alignment character-istic of the Fermi statistics.

Although the Landau theory accounts for all the main features of the liquid, there still remain points for further discussion. The theory predicts that various properties of the liquid should show the same dependence on temperature as those of a degenerate perfect gas. Hence at sufficiently low temperatures the specific heat should be directly proportional to the temperature, and we might expect to observe this behaviour below about 50 mK. Measurements in this region are difficult, but show that the specific heat, and also the thermal conductivity, vary rather less rapidly with temperature than is expected, even below 10 mK (see for example reference [19]). These results suggest that the Landau treatment as given above is in need of some modification or extension.

The need for some modification is also suggested when we consider the properties of the liquid between about 1 K and

50 mK. In this region, liquid ³He exhibits a gradual transition from its high-temperature classical behaviour to the degenerate Fermi behaviour, and it would be of interest to obtain a satisfactory theoretical account of this transition. Yet it does not seem possible to deduce these properties directly from the Landau model. A recent approach to this problem has been to introduce another feature into the treatment, the so-called paramagnons.

We saw in section 3.3 that the exchange forces in liquid ³He tend to align the ³He nuclei in a ferromagnetic arrangement, in opposition to the rather larger effect of the Fermi statistics, which leads to an anti-parallel alignment. In fact if the exchange forces were 50 per cent stronger the liquid would be a nuclear ferromagnetic. Hence it has been proposed by Doniach and Engelsberg that, because of fluctuations, small regions in the liquid will momentarily take up ferromagnetic arrangements. The fluctuations are then regarded as additional excitations in the liquid, the 'paramagnons'. The presence of these paramagnons modifies the entropy of the liquid, and hence all its thermodynamic properties. They will also scatter the quasi-particles in transport processes, and so modify the kinetic coefficients. For a review of the present position see reference [20].

4.2. Liquid ³He and superconductivity

All the treatments mentioned in the previous section assume that liquid ³He can be described by perturbation theory from a perfect gas model. However the BCS theory of superconductivity (see for example reference [21]) shows that under certain conditions the ground state of a system cannot be deduced in this way. The electrons in a superconducting metal form the so-called Cooper pairs to give a correlated phase, and the resulting ground-state energy is less than any that can be obtained from perturbation theory. Although liquid ³He is obviously quite a different system from the electron gas in a metal, the BCS theory of superconductivity has been generalized to deal with other systems of interacting fermions. As a result, several authors have suggested that, at sufficiently low temperatures, liquid ³He might exhibit a transition to some form of correlated phase.

These treatments usually characterize the interactions in the liquid by the potential function for two interacting ³He atoms. It appears that a transition to a correlated or super-conducting phase is to be expected provided that the inter-action between the atoms is not dominated by the repulsive part of the potential. That is, there must be a region in which the interaction is essentially attractive. In some of the first papers on this problem it was assumed that the relative motion of two atoms in liquid ³He could be adequately represented by S state wave functions. In this case the repulsive terms predominate, and a phase transition is not expected.

It was next pointed out that a more complete representation of the relative motion of two atoms in the liquid is obtained by expanding the motion in terms of all the possible two-particle states. That is, the motion should be resolved into components corresponding both to S and to P, D, and higher states. Calcu-lations show that the attractive part of the potential is dominant in the D state, so that a transition to a correlated condition is predicted for this component.

The calculations involved in this discussion indicate the very severe difficulties involved in solving the many-body problem to obtain numerical values which are correct to even an order of magnitude. Thus the first estimates of the transition temperature lay between 0·05 and 0·15 K, but these had to be revised in the light of later experimental evidence, which gave no sign of any transition in this region. Subsequent estimates of the order of 0·02 K were again revised after further experi-ments. The physical properties of ³He have now been ob-served down to 3 millikelvins, and show no sign of a transition (save for one set of specific heat measurements which are almost certainly spurious). At present the revised estimate for the transition temperature lies between 10^{-4} and 10^{-3} K, a region not very easy to reach experimentally.

The problem of deciding whether liquid ³He should become superfluid illustrates the difficulties attending much of the theory mentioned in this chapter. The main technique for the evaluation of the eigenvalues of a system of interacting particles is perturbation theory. To obtain useful results, approximations have to be made, but it is hard to decide what approximations are fully justified. In discussing superconducting metals, one is aided in selecting the correct approximations by a knowledge of the transition temperatures. However this information is not available for liquid ³He.

Several authors refer to the predicted low-temperature condition as a *superfluid* phase. This is an unsatisfactory term, in no way to be identified with the superfluid properties of liquid ⁴He. In fact, the discussions only suggest that the viscosity may depend on the velocity gradient, and fall below the value given by the $1/T^2$ temperature dependence of the Landau theory. The specific heat immediately below the transition might be augmented by a factor 2, and the susceptibility reduced by about 10 per cent. There is no suggestion that the liquid could flow through a capillary with zero viscosity.

4.3. Solutions of ³He in liquid ⁴He

The behaviour of dilute solutions of ³He in liquid ⁴He below about 0·5 K gives important information on the Fermi liquid. This comes about because the heat motion in liquid ⁴He has then almost completely disappeared, its entropy and specific heat being very much less than that of liquid ³He. Hence the liquid ⁴He in the solution behaves only as a 'background fluid', in which the ³He atoms move about rather as a gas of atoms in a vacuum. However, as a moving ³He atom has to push aside ⁴He atoms, the true inertial mass m_3 of the ³He atoms must be replaced by a larger effective mass m_3^*. (We discuss these points in more detail in section 10.3).

As we may largely disregard the presence of the ⁴He atoms in a ³He–⁴He solution at low temperatures, we expect the ³He atoms to be described by the Fermi liquid theory.

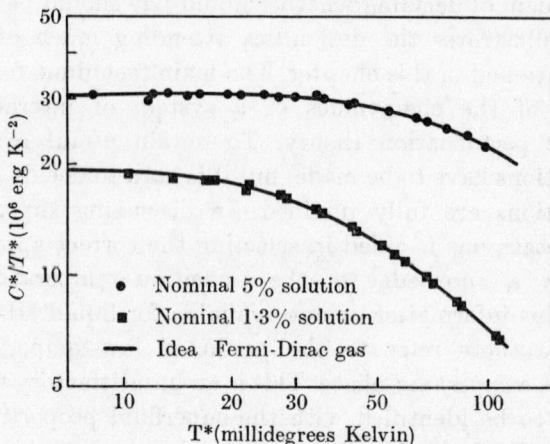

FIG. 4.1. The ratio of the thermal capacity C^* to the temperature T^* of two dilute solutions of ^{3}He in helium II each containing 0·50 moles of helium (Anderson, Roach, Sarwinski, and Wheatley [22]).

Moreover, as the atoms in dilute solutions are well separated, the interactions between them will be weak, and so we expect their behaviour to approximate to that of a perfect Fermi gas. This is in fact observed. We show in section 10.1 that above 0·5 K the specific heat of the ^{3}He atoms is equal to $\frac{3}{2}k_B$ per atom, as for a perfect gas. However, at lower temperatures, it falls below this value and eventually becomes linear in the temperature, as may be seen for 1·3% and 5% solutions in Fig. 4.1. At the lowest temperatures, the specific heat has the value we would expect if the effective mass of the ^{3}He atoms was equal to $2·4\,m_3$, where m_3 is the atomic mass, in fair agreement with estimates obtained in other ways. The full lines in the figure show the calculated values of the specific heat of a degenerate perfect gas of the same number density, and we see that it coincides closely with the measured points.

The magnetic susceptibility of dilute solutions down to at least 0·35 K exhibits the temperature dependence which we would calculate for a Fermi gas with an effective mass of $2·5$ m_3. Measurements have also been made of the thermal conductivity of dilute solutions. At temperatures of a few millikelvins the conductivity varies almost exactly as the inverse of the temperature, as we would expect for a perfect gas in the Fermi limit. We conclude that we are observing a degenerate Fermi system with relatively weak interactions, and which should therefore be susceptible to accurate calculations. Moreover, by diluting liquid ^{3}He with ^{4}He, we can pass from a strongly interacting assembly of ^{3}He atoms to one which behaves rather as a perfect gas. Hence we have the possibly of making experiments on a liquid ^{3}He of variable number density, and with different strengths of interactions. Note, however, that the derivation of the transport and other kinetic properties is somewhat complicated by the presence of the ^{4}He atoms (see for example reference [23]).

4.4. The melting curve

The melting curve of ^{3}He has the same general form as that of ^{4}He, except that the melting pressure exhibits a shallow minimum of about 29 atm in the region of 0·3 K, as shown in Fig. 4.2. This minimum has interesting implications. Consider

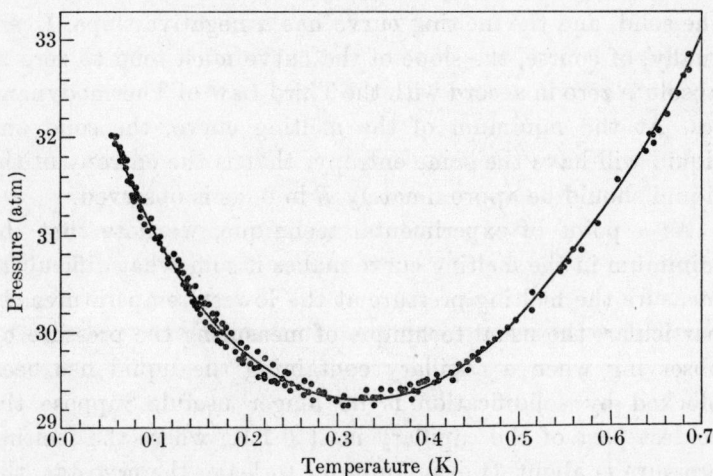

FIG. 4.2. The melting curve of ^{3}He (Edwards, Baum, Brewer, Daunt, and McWilliams [24]).

the Clausius Clapeyron relation

$$\left(\frac{\partial P}{\partial T}\right)_{\text{melt}} = \frac{S_1 - S_{\text{s}}}{V_1 - V_{\text{s}}},$$

where S and V are the molar entropies and volumes, and the subscripts 1 and s refer to the liquid and solid. The volume increase on melting is quite large, and remains so at the lowest temperatures. Hence the rise of the curve below 0·3 K ($dP/dT < 0$) implies that the entropy of the solid is greater than that of the liquid.

The above behaviour comes about because the atoms in the solid are more localized than in the liquid; their wave functions overlap less, and the exchange forces are correspondingly smaller. Hence the spins in the solid remain unaligned down to well below 0·01 K. Above this temperature, the entropy of the solid must therefore include a contribution of $R \ln 2$ from the spin disorder. Moreover, as the lattice entropy is very small below 1 K, the total entropy of the solid will be quite close to $R \ln 2$. In the liquid, the spin disorder is removed at much higher temperatures, and the entropy drops off rapidly. Hence the entropy of the liquid finally becomes less than that of the solid, and the melting curve has a negative slope. Eventually, of course, the slope of the curve must tend to zero at absolute zero in accord with the Third Law of Thermodynamics. At the minimum of the melting curve, the solid and liquid will have the same entropy, that is the entropy of the liquid should be approximately $R \ln 2$, as is observed.

As a point of experimental technique, we note that the minimum in the melting curve makes it somewhat difficult to measure the melting pressure at the lowest temperatures. In particular, the usual technique of measuring the pressure by observing when a capillary containing the liquid has been blocked by solidification is no longer useful. Suppose the coldest part of the capillary is at 0·1 K, where the melting pressure is about 31 atm. In order to leave the cryostat, the capillary must somewhere pass through a temperature of 0·3 K, where the melting pressure is only about 29 atm.

Hence, if the specimen is at a temperature below 0·3 K, the capillary will always block at about 29 atm. It is therefore necessary to work with a fixed volume of ³He and measure the pressure either with strain gauges or with some form of bellows device.

A corollary of Fig. 4.2 is provided by detailed measurements on the melting curve of ⁴He. To a first approximation the

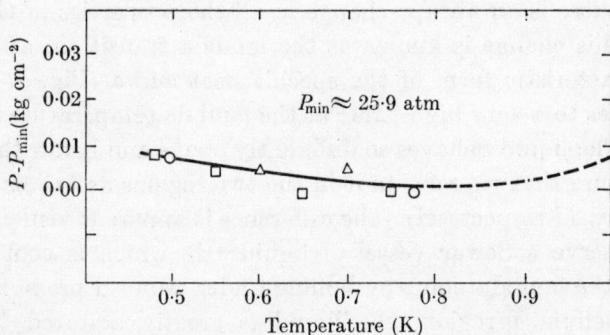

FIG. 4.3. The melting pressure P of ⁴He at low temperature, expressed as $(P - P_m)$ versus T, where P_m is the pressure at the minimum (after Le Pair, Taconis, De Bruyn Ouboter, and Das [25]).

melting curve is independent of pressure below 0·1 K (section 1.2). However very sensitive measurements on ⁴He contained in the tube of a bourdon type gauge show the presence of an extremely shallow minimum at about 0·8 K (Fig. 4.3). To account for this minimum, we note that below 0·6 K the entropies of both the liquid and solid arise almost entirely from phonon excitations (see section 7.2). Only longitudinal modes are possible in the liquid, whereas the solid can support both a longitudinal and two transverse modes. Hence, we may calculate from the usual Debye theory that, at the lowest temperatures, the solid will have the greater entropy, so the melting curve must exhibit a minimum. As the entropies involved are small, the gradient of the melting curve given by the Clausius-Clapeyron relation is also small, and the minimum very shallow. Eventually, of course, the slope will tend to zero.

CHAPTER V

LIQUID HELIUM II

LIKE liquid ^{3}He at higher temperatures, liquid ^{4}He near its boiling point may be regarded as behaving rather like a dense gas of classical particles. However, at a temperature of 2·17 K, there is an abrupt change in all the properties of the liquid. This change is known as the lambda transition, after the characteristic form of the specific heat curve (Fig. 1.3), which rises to a very high value at the lambda temperature of 2·17 K. The liquid behaves so differently above and below this temperature that we refer to it in the two regions as *helium I* and *helium II* respectively. The difference is apparent visually if we observe a dewar vessel of liquid ^{4}He which is cooled through the lambda point by boiling under reduced pressure. In the helium I region, the liquid is greatly agitated by bubbles of vapour which form throughout the liquid. Yet, immediately the lambda point is passed, the liquid becomes quite calm and still. Further investigation shows that heat transport takes place so readily within the fluid that it is almost impossible to set up appreciable temperature gradients; hence all the evaporation takes place from the free surface, without bubbling.

5.1. Viscosity and superfluidity

Measurements of the flow of helium II through very fine capillaries indicate a vanishingly small viscosity, at least 10^6 times smaller than that of helium I. This is the so-called *superfluidity* of liquid helium II, perhaps its most characteristic feature. For not too great pressures, the velocity of flow through these fine capillaries appears independent of the pressure head, and is actually *greater* in tubes of *smaller* diameter.

The viscosity has also been measured with rotation viscometers. The results are quite dissimilar from those described

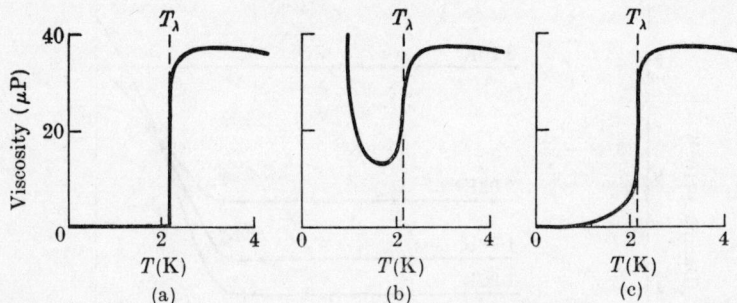

FIG. 5.1. The apparent viscosity of liquid ^{4}He measured (a) by a Poiseuille flow method, (b) in a rotation viscometer, (c) in an oscillating disc viscometer.

above; in particular there appears to be no difficulty in observing a normal coefficient of viscosity. Fig. 5.1(b) shows values of the viscosity obtained in this way; the magnitude is of the same order as that observed in helium I, although the dependence on temperature is different. Fig. 5.1(c) shows values of the viscosity deduced in the usual way from the damping on a disc oscillating in the liquid. For conventional liquids, including liquid helium I, we expect to obtain the same values for the viscosity in both a rotation and oscillation viscometer, but Fig. 5 shows that this is not so for helium II.

A characteristic feature of the behaviour of helium II is illustrated in Fig. 5.2, which shows the damping on an oscillating disc as a function of the amplitude of the oscillations. The damping is independent of amplitude over a large range of amplitude, and then rapidly increases, rather as if some form of turbulence had set in quite abruptly. We return to this point in section 5·3.

Associated with superfluidity is the behaviour exhibited in the remarkable beaker experiment illustrated in Fig. 5.3. A small beaker or test tube containing helium II is suspended above a bath of helium II at the same temperature. It is observed that the liquid in the beaker falls to a lower level by flowing up and over the edge of the beaker, then down to the bottom of the tube, where it forms drops which fall off into the bath.

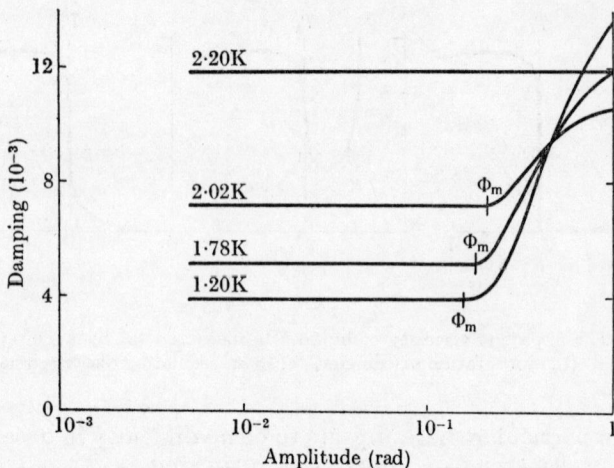

FIG. 5.2. The damping on a disc oscillating in liquid helium II, as a function
of the amplitude of oscillation (Hollis Hallett [26]).

5.2. The thermomechanical effect

Another property is illustrated by the simple experiment of
Fig. 5.4. A and B are two vessels joined by a fine capillary.
Initially both vessels contain helium II, at the same temper-
ature, and standing at the same level. If an excess pressure

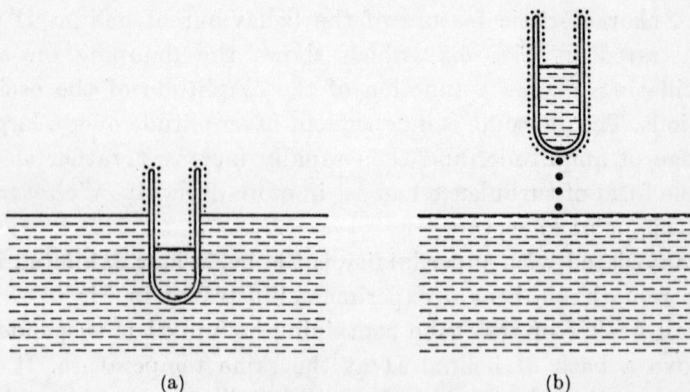

(a)   (b)

FIG. 5.3. (a) If an empty beaker is lowered into a bath of helium II, the
liquid flows over the surface of the beaker until the levels are equalized.
(b) If the beaker is then lifted above the bath, the helium flows out over the
rim, drops off the bottom of the beaker, and returns to the bath (after Daunt
and Mendelssohn [27]).

ΔP is applied over the helium in vessel A, liquid flows through the capillary into the vessel B, where the level will stand above that in A. In addition, however, the temperature of A rises a little, and that of B falls. Moreover, on releasing the excess pressure, the system returns to its original condition. This result implies, unequivocally, that the liquid which passes through the capillary is different from the bulk

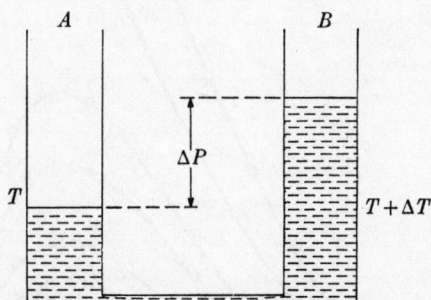

FIG. 5.4. The vessels A and B are joined by a fine capillary. A displacement of liquid helium II from A to B creates a temperature difference between the two vessels. Alternatively, a temperature difference ΔT results in a hydrostatic pressure difference ΔP.

liquid in the vessels A and B. In fact, the properties of helium II are often described in terms of a 'two-fluid model', the liquid being regarded as the sum of two 'fluids', one of which flows through the capillary while the other does not. In another version of this experiment we start with the helium in vessels A and B, at the same level and the same temperature, and then raise the temperature of one vessel by a small amount ΔT. We then observe a change in level corresponding to a pressure change ΔP, the relative magnitudes of ΔP and ΔT being similar to those observed previously. This phenomenon is known as the thermomechanical effect, but is also sometimes referred to as the fountain effect, because so much heat was supplied in one of the earliest experiments, that the liquid was thrown up in a jet.

4

5.3. Heat transport

The behaviour of the flow of heat in helium II is also remarkable. As the transfer of heat is very high, many measurements have been made in long narrow glass capillaries, any heat flow in the glass being negligible compared with that in the helium.

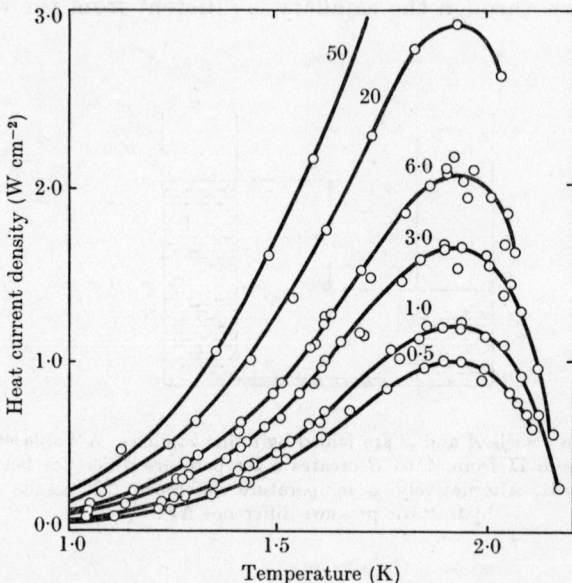

FIG. 5.5. The heat current density produced by different temperature gradients in capillaries of the order of 1 mm diameter. The numbers on each curve give the temperature gradient in 10^{-3} K cm^{-1} (after Keesom, Saris, and Meyer [28]).

Some early results are shown in Fig. 5.5. The heat flow is very high, passes through a maximum at about 1·8 K, and appears to be proportional to $(dT/dx)^{\frac{1}{3}}$, the cube root of the temperature gradient. Clearly we are dealing with a very complicated phenomenon. However, if measurements are made with not too large heat flows, in very narrow channels, then the flow is proportional to the temperature gradient. For example Fig. 5.6 shows some results where the heat flow is proportional to the temperature difference up to a certain value, but then increases less rapidly. Even in this linear region, however, the heat flow is far from normal. It is extemely high, and not proportional to the area of the slit.

In order to discuss the complex behaviour of helium II in detail it is convenient to consider various patterns of behaviour separately. We have just seen that at sufficiently low velocities the damping on an oscillating disc is independent of

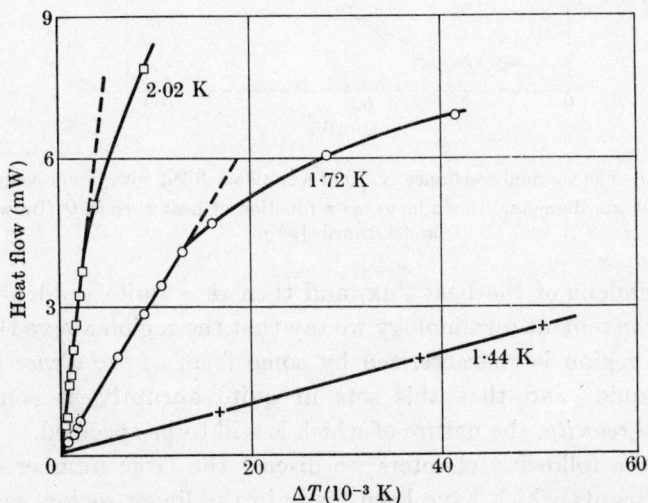

FIG. 5.6. The heat flow through liquid helium in a slit of width 2·4 μm as a function of the temperature difference ΔT across the slit. The relation is linear for small heat flows at not too high temperatures (after Winkel, Groenou, and Gorter [29]).

velocity, and the heat flow is proportional to the applied temperature difference. In fact, it is found that in a wide range of experiments, similar linear relations are valid, provided that the fluxes of heat or momentum are not too large. We shall describe this condition of the liquid as the *linear region*. As is suggested by Fig. 5.2, this region is not to be regarded as one in which the additional effects observed at higher fluxes are small, but rather as one in which they are entirely absent. This point is emphasized by measurements on the flow of heat in a capillary 10 cm long and about 0·1 mm in diameter (Fig. 5.7). The thermal resistance of the liquid is initially

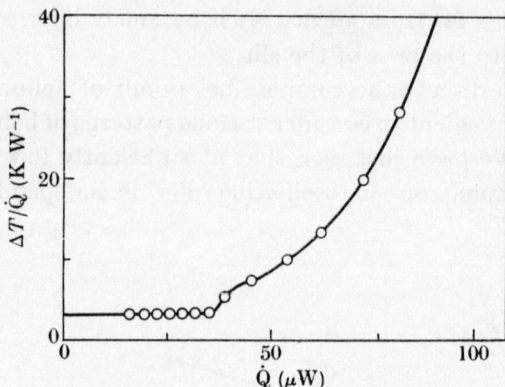

FIG. 5.7. The thermal resistance $\Delta T/\dot{Q}$ of a capillary filled with liquid helium II (107·6 μm diameter, 10 cm long), as a function of heat current $\dot{Q}$ (Brewer and Edwards [30]).

independent of the heat flux, and then rises quite suddenly. As a convenient terminology we say that the region above the linear region is characterized by some form of *turbulence* in the liquid, and that this sets in quite abruptly at some *critical velocity*, the nature of which is still to be specified.

In the following chapters we discuss the large number of experiments which have been made in the linear region, and their interpretation in terms of a 'two-fluid' model. The behaviour of helium II in the turbulent region turns out to be intimately related to the fact that many of its kinetic properties are modified when the liquid is set in rotation. This we discuss in Chapters 12 to 14.

5.4. Second sound

One of the most unusual features of helium II is that variations of temperature propagate through the liquid not according to the usual Fourier equation, but as a true wave motion whose velocity is independent of the frequency. These temperature waves are entirely analogous to ordinary sound waves, save that the thermodynamic variable is temperature and not pressure. Thus we can excite temperature waves with a heater in a resonance tube, and detect standing waves using a thermometer as a detector, as shown in Fig. 5.8. Alternatively this wave-like transmission of heat enables us to transmit sharp pulses of temperature as compact pulses through the liquid. This very unusual type of heat propagation is known as second sound. The name is not a particularly

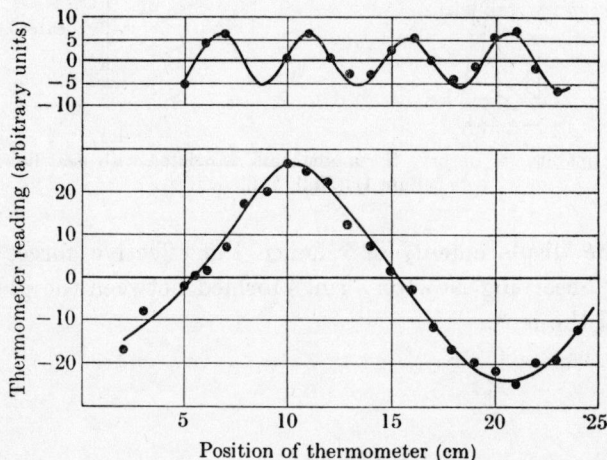

FIG. 5.8. Typical standing wave patterns of second sound (Peshkov [31]).

good one, but has arisen for historical reasons which we touch on in section 6.3.

5.5. The momentum of heat flow

The flow of heat in helium II is accompanied by a flow of momentum. This momentum was first observed by Kapitza, who showed that a heat current impinging on a vane mounted on a torsion wire gave rise to a pressure which deflected the vane. A later experimental arrangement is shown schematically in Fig. 5.9. A flat heater wound from thin wire is mounted on one side of a thin glass plate suspended close to a convex lens, the whole assembly being immersed in a bath of helium. The low conductivity of the glass plate ensures that virtually all the heat flow from the wires takes place uni-directionally down the tube t; the plate therefore tends to move to the

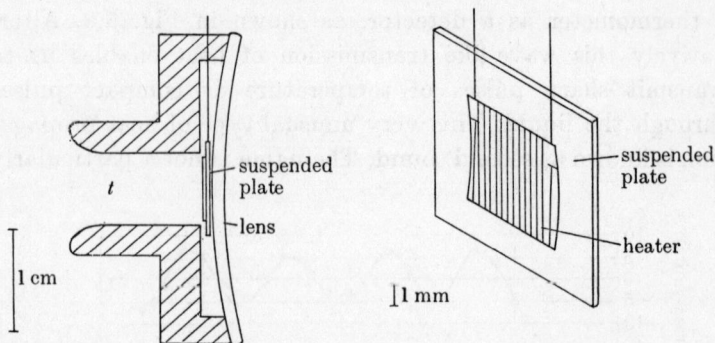

FIG. 5.9. Apparatus to observe the momentum associated with heat flow in helium II (Hall [32]).

right. The displacement, and hence the effective force, is found by observing Newton's rings formed between the glass plate and the lens.

CHAPTER VI

THE TWO-FLUID PROPERTIES OF HELIUM II

UNTIL Chapter 13, we shall confine our attention to experiments in which the heat and mass currents are not too large. That is, we shall deal with helium II in the well-defined *linear region* mentioned in section 5.3. It turns out that, in this region, many of the unusual properties of the liquid may be correlated with each other, and with the thermodynamic functions, by a mathematical picture known as the 'two-fluid model'.

6.1. The two-fluid model

The two-fluid model postulates that liquid helium II behaves as if it were a mixture of two fluids freely intermingling with each other without any viscous interaction.

These two fluids are termed the *normal fluid* and the *super-fluid*, and have densities ρ_n and ρ_s such that

$$\rho_n + \rho_s = \rho, \qquad (6.1)$$

where ρ is the ordinary density of liquid helium. The normal density ρ_n is a function of temperature, and *increases from zero at absolute zero, to the value ρ at the lambda point*. Conversely, the superfluid density is zero at the lambda point and increases to the value ρ at temperature zero.

In addition, the model postulates that the superfluid carries zero entropy, and experiences no resistance whatever to its flow, that is, it exhibits neither viscosity nor turbulence. This condition is specified by stipulating that the viscosity of the superfluid is zero, and that its velocity $\mathbf{v}_s$ satisfies the relation

$$\operatorname{curl} \mathbf{v}_s = 0.$$

On the other hand the normal fluid has a viscosity, the so-called *normal viscosity* η_n, and an entropy S_n equal to the entropy of the liquid helium. Thus the essential parameters of the model are shown in the following table.

Normal fluid	ρ_n	$\eta = \eta_n$	$S_n = S_{He}$
Superfluid	ρ_s	$\eta = 0$	$S_s = 0.$

The parameters ρ_n and ρ_s, and η_n, are functions of temperature but, at a given temperature, are taken as constants of the model. Their values as functions of temperature are deduced from some of the experiments described in the following sections. After these parameters have been determined, the model then correlates a wide variety of experimental results, without introducing any additional terms or adjustable constants. (The total density ρ also varies slightly with temperature, but the variation is very small, and to a good approximation may be ignored.)

We must stress that our use of the model only implies that helium II behaves *as if it were* a mixture of two fluids. It does *not* imply that helium II is a mixture of two real physical fluids. The liquid is an assembly of ^{4}He atoms which are all identical. We discuss how the mathematical model arises from physical principles in Chapters 7 and 8.

6.2. The equations of motion

We now derive equations of motion for the two fluids of the model, as given by Landau [33]. Let the symbol $\mathbf{j}$ denote the momentum of unit volume of liquid helium, and $\mathbf{v_n}$ and $\mathbf{v_s}$ the velocities of the two fluids, then

$$\mathbf{j} = \rho_n\mathbf{v_n} + \rho_s\mathbf{v_s}. \tag{6.2}$$

The flow $\mathbf{j}$ is also related to the density of the helium by the equation of continuity

$$\operatorname{div}\mathbf{j} = -\frac{\partial\rho}{\partial t}. \tag{6.3}$$

If the velocities of the two fluids are small as is often the case, we may ignore viscous effects and terms quadratic in the velocities. Euler's standard equation of motion then reduces to

$$\frac{\partial\mathbf{j}}{\partial t} = -\operatorname{grad} P, \tag{6.4}$$

where P is the pressure.

In the approximation which ignores the viscosity, the motions of the two fluids are reversible so that entropy is conserved. Thus, bearing in mind that the entropy of the liquid is associated only with the normal fluid, we have

$$\frac{\partial(\rho S)}{\partial t} = -\operatorname{div}(\rho S\mathbf{v_n}), \tag{6.5}$$

where S is the entropy per g of liquid, and ρS the entropy per unit volume.

Finally we need an equation for the forces acting on the superfluid alone, and therefore write down the usual differential expression for the change in the internal energy of a mass of liquid helium when a change is made in the entropy, volume, and mass,

$$dU = T\,dS - P\,dV + G\,dM.$$

In this expression G is the Gibbs free energy of one gramme of liquid, i.e. the chemical potential, and dM is a change in the mass of the assembly. Let us now increase the mass of the assembly at constant volume by introducing particles which contribute only to the ground state, that is to the superfluid. As dS = dV = 0, it follows that the increase in internal energy is G dM. Hence the work done in transfering a mass ΔM of superfluid from a point 1 in the liquid to an adjacent point 2 a distance dx away is

$$\Delta W = (G_2 - G_1)\,\Delta M = \text{grad}\;G\,.\,\mathrm{d}x\,.\,\Delta M.$$

It follows that the equation of motion of the superfluid may be written

$$\frac{\mathrm{d}\mathbf{v}_s}{\mathrm{d}t} = -\text{grad}\;G.$$

Expressing grad G in terms of standard thermodynamic identities, and again ignoring terms quadratic in the velocities, the last equation becomes

$$\frac{\partial \mathbf{v}_s}{\partial t} = S\;\text{grad}\;T - \frac{1}{\rho}\;\text{grad}\;P. \tag{6.6}$$

Equations (6.1) to (6.6) are the basic equations of the two-fluid model in the linear approximation. We now apply them to the properties of helium II.

6.3. Second sound

Equations (6.3) and (6.4) lead readily to the relation

$$\frac{\partial^2 p}{\partial x^2} = \frac{1}{c^2}\frac{\partial^2 p}{\partial t^2},$$

the usual equation for the propagation of density or pressure changes in a liquid. However, there is the additional possibility, with the two-fluid model, of a fluctuation in the relative densities of the normal and superfluids, while the total density $(\rho_s + \rho_n)$ remains constant. As a change in the relative densities of normal and superfluids is equivalent to a change in temperature, an oscillation of the two fluids relative to each other corresponds to an entirely new phenomenon, a true oscillation of temperature. Remembering that the thermal expansion coefficient of helium is small, we can solve the five equations of the model and obtain the ordinary sound equation as before, plus a second relation

$$\frac{\partial^2 S}{\partial x^2} = \frac{\rho_n}{\rho_s}\frac{C}{TS^2}\frac{\partial^2 S}{\partial t^2},$$

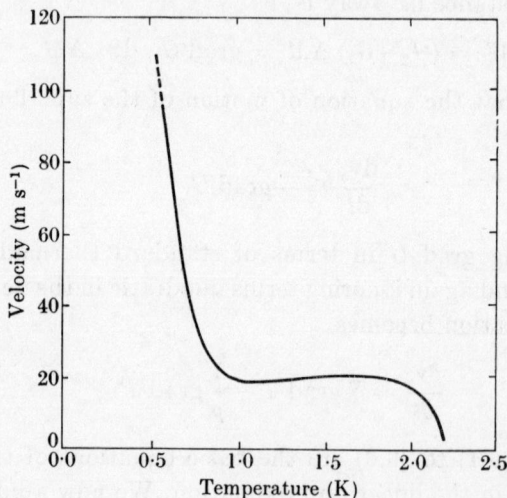

FIG. 6.1. The velocity of second sound (after Peshkov [31]).

C being the specific heat of unit mass of helium. This is a wave equation for the propagation of variations of entropy, or, what amounts to the same thing, variations of temperature. Thus the model predicts the existence of harmonic temperature waves with a velocity

$$c_2 = \left(\frac{\rho_s}{\rho_n}\frac{TS^2}{C}\right)^{\frac{1}{2}}.$$

The velocity has been measured both by standing wave and pulse techniques, and some results are shown in Fig. 6.1. From these values we may deduce values of ρ_n which are in good agreement with those obtained from other methods described below, see Fig. 6.2. In fact, measurements of the velocity give the most accurate method of determining ρ_n. (Fig. 6.1 suggests that the velocity rises indefinitely below 1 K In fact, below about 0·6 K, we expect it to take up a steady value equal to the velocity of ordinary sound divided by $\sqrt{3}$,

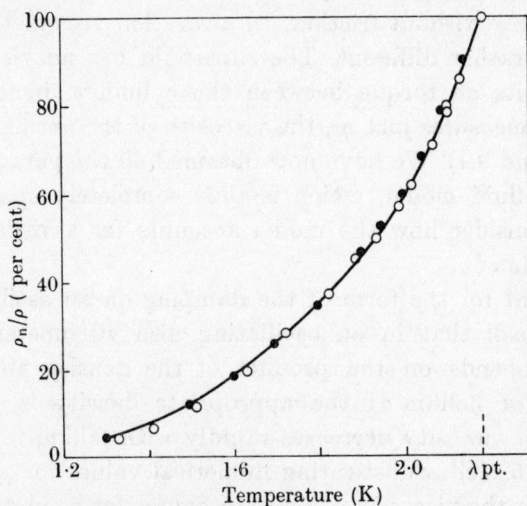

Fig. 6.2. The density of the normal fluid ρ_n as a function of temperature: O derived from oscillating disc experiments, ● from the velocity of second sound (Andronikashvili [34]).

or about 140 m s^{-1}. However, as we explain in section 8.5, it is generally difficult to observe second sound in this region.)

Historically, it should be mentioned that the existence of temperature waves was first predicted by Tisza on the basis of a different and less satisfactory model. However, at the time of writing his first paper, Landau was apparently unaware of this work, and seems to have thought that the velocity c_2 would be associated with sound of the usual type but with another velocity—hence he gave it the name 'second sound'. It was only after a failure to excite such waves with a piezo-electric crystal, that it was realized that a much more effective technique would be to generate a periodically varying temperature.

6.4. The viscosity

We now use the model to explain the very different values of the viscosity given by three standard methods of measurement (Fig. 5.1). In a Poiseuille flow type of measurement, the motion of the normal fluid is restricted by its viscosity, but the superfluid moves readily with zero viscosity. Hence we observe a flow without friction. In a rotation viscometer the position is rather different. The superfluid has no viscosity and transmits no torque between the cylinders, hence the viscometer measures just η_n, the viscosity of the normal fluid (Figs. 5.1 and 9.1). We have now obtained all the parameters of the two-fluid model, which is thus completely specified. We next consider how the model accounts for a variety of other phenomena.

To account for the form of the damping on an oscillating disc, we recall that in an oscillating disc viscometer, the damping depends on the product of the density and the viscosity. For helium II the appropriate density is ρ_n, so the *apparent* viscosity decreases rapidly with falling temperature (Fig. 5.1(c)). Substituting numerical values for ρ_n and recalculating the viscosity, we obtain figures for η_n in reasonable agreement with those given by the rotation viscometer.

We note also that the beaker experiment illustrated in Fig. 5.3 is readily explained in terms of the superfluidity of the helium. The exposed surfaces of the beaker are in equilibrium with the saturated vapour of the liquid in the bath, and will therefore be covered with a film of adsorbed helium, which is of the order of 200 Å thick. This film forms a continuous link between the two levels of helium in Fig. 5.3. Moreover the helium II forming the film can flow in narrow channels as a superfluid without any friction. Hence the film acts as a form of syphon between the helium in the beaker and the bath, so the two levels tend to equalize. Thus the motion of helium provides one more example of a liquid, albeit a quantum liquid, finding its own level! We should perhaps point out that there is no particular mystery as to the nature of the driving force for the motion. It is the difference in

gravitational potential which leads to a difference in the free
energy of the two liquids. As the levels are linked by the film
they tend to adjust themselves until their free energies are
equal.

6.5. Andronikashvili's experiment

This experiment gives the most direct method of measuring
the density of the normal fluid ρ_n. It uses an apparatus rather

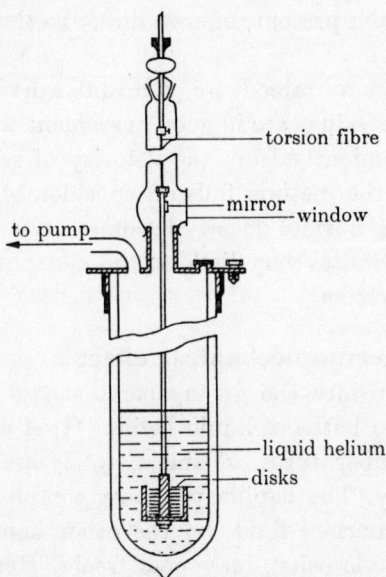

FIG. 6.3. Schematic diagram to illustrate Andronikashvili's experiment.
Note that the discs are not drawn to scale; see text (Andronikashvili [34]).

similar to an oscillating disc viscometer except that the
oscillating disc is replaced by a cylindrical vessel, in which is
rigidly fixed a pile of fifty thin metal discs, as shown schematically in Fig. 6.3. This whole unit is mounted on a fine torsion
suspension so that it can oscillate in liquid helium with a
period of about 30 seconds. According to the two-fluid model,
the superfluid takes no part in this motion, but normal fluid is
dragged round by the discs as in the oscillation viscometer.

The penetration depth for a viscous wave, of angular frequency ω, in a liquid of density ρ_n and viscosity η_n is of the order of $(2\eta_n/\rho_n\omega)^{\frac{1}{2}}$, and at all temperatures below the lambda point this distance is appreciably greater than the spacing between the discs. Hence *all* the normal fluid between the discs is dragged round with them. Since the mass of this normal fluid varies with temperature, the apparent moment of inertia, and therefore the period of the system, also varies with temperature. Thus a measurement of the period, with and without helium present, offers a direct method of determining ρ_n.

The results obtained by Andronikashvili are shown in Fig. 6.2. The values are in good agreement with those derived quite independently from the velocity of second sound. The accuracy of the method falls off considerably at low temperatures, as the normal density becomes very small, so that the helium contributes very little to the moment of inertia of the oscillating system.

6.6. The thermomechanical effect

Let us consider the arrangement shown schematically in Fig. 5.4. Two baths of liquid helium II, A and B, at slightly different temperatures, T and $T+\Delta T$, are connected by a fine capillary. The capillary almost completely inhibits any flow of the normal fluid; on the other hand the superfluid, having zero viscosity, may pass freely. Hence the capillary acts as a form of semi-permeable membrane. Therefore, as the concentration of normal fluid is somewhat greater in the hotter bath, an osmotic pressure is set up, and superfluid tends to flow from A to B to equalize the concentrations in the two baths. This flow continues until the osmotic pressure is balanced by the resulting excess hydrostatic pressure ΔP.

The magnitude of the effect follows directly from the two-fluid model. In equilibrium there is no acceleration of the superfluid in the capillary, hence according to equation (6.6)

$$\frac{\partial \mathbf{v}_s}{\partial t} = S \operatorname{grad} T - \frac{1}{\rho} \operatorname{grad} P = 0,$$

it follows that

$$\frac{\Delta P}{\Delta T} = \rho S, \tag{6.7}$$

a result first given by H. London. The effect is very large; for example at 1·5 K a temperature difference of only one milli-kelvin produces a pressure head of about 2 cm of liquid helium.

The fountain effect implies that if we let helium II run out of a container through a fine capillary, the emerging liquid will all be superfluid at temperature zero. In fact the outflowing liquid is never at absolute zero, as there will always be some flow of normal fluid in a capillary of finite diameter. However, a very considerable cooling of the emerging liquid is observed, while the temperature of the remaining liquid rises. Note that this method of producing very low temperatures is not of much practical use, as below 1 K the helium has very little entropy, and therefore very little capacity to cool other substances.

6.7. Heat transport

We consider the two reservoirs of helium at temperatures T and $T + \Delta T$ which were shown in Fig. 5.4. These two reservoirs are connected by a narrow capillary across which is developed a fountain pressure $\Delta P = \rho S \, \Delta T$. When discussing the fountain effect, we assumed the capillary to be infinitely narrow, but in fact it will allow some flow of the normal fluid under the action of the pressure ΔP. Hence, even in equilibrium conditions, there will be a steady flow of normal fluid from the hot to the cold reservoir, and a return flow of super-fluid to conserve mass. As the normal fluid carries all the entropy, and the superfluid none, the net effect of this flow is to transfer entropy from the hot to the cold reservoir. This entropy transfer manifests itself as a large flux of heat.

The rates of flow of the two fluids in the capillary are limited only by the viscosity of the normal fluid. The volume rate of flow of this component is given by Poiseuille's formula to be

$$\dot{V}_n = \frac{\beta}{\eta_n} \frac{\Delta P}{\Delta x}, \tag{6.8}$$

where Δx is the length of the channel, and β a constant depending on its geometry. Since the superfluid carries no entropy, the rate of entropy transport between the reservoirs is $\dot{V}_n(\rho S)$. Hence, assuming as usual that the motion of the two fluids is reversible, the heat flow $\dot{Q} = T(\dot{V}_n \rho S)$. Substituting (6.8) into this expression, and using the London relation (6.7) for the fountain pressure, we finally obtain

$$\dot{Q} = \frac{\beta T (\rho S)^2}{\eta_n} \frac{\Delta T}{\Delta x}. \tag{6.9}$$

The verification of equation (6.9) is not entirely simple, as temperature differences of only a few millikelvins produce large fluxes of heat. Also the constant β contains the fourth power of the radius of the capillary (or the third power of the width of a rectangular slit). However, careful measurements have now shown that the relation is correct to within at least a few parts per cent. That is, the viscosity η_n can be correctly deduced from measurements of the heat flow. Note that the relation involves no adjustable constants.

Finally we note that, in the linear region, the heat flow for a given temperature gradient steadily increases with rising temperature right up to the lambda point in agreement with equation (6.9). The maximum in the apparent conductivity shown in Fig. 5.5 is only characteristic of higher heat flows in the nonlinear region which we consider in Chapter 13.

6.8. The momentum of heat flow

As we have seen in the previous section, the flow of heat in helium II is accompanied by motion of the two fluids. Therefore, as the two fluids have momentum, the two-fluid model predicts that a flux of heat is accompanied by fluxes of momentum. This is the momentum already referred to in section 5.5. The momentum flux associated with each fluid has the form $\rho \mathbf{v} \cdot \mathbf{v}$; thus in a unidirectional flow of heat there is a reaction pressure

$$P = \rho_n v_n^2 + \rho_s v_s^2$$

on the source due to the inertia of the fluids. The heat flow per unit area $W = \rho S T v_{\mathrm{n}}$, and in the absence of mass flow $\rho_{\mathrm{n}} v_{\mathrm{n}} + \rho_{\mathrm{s}} v_{\mathrm{s}} = 0$, hence

$$P = \frac{\rho_{\mathrm{n}} W^2}{\rho_{\mathrm{s}} \rho T^2 S^2} = \frac{W^2}{c_2^2 \rho C T}, \qquad (6.10)$$

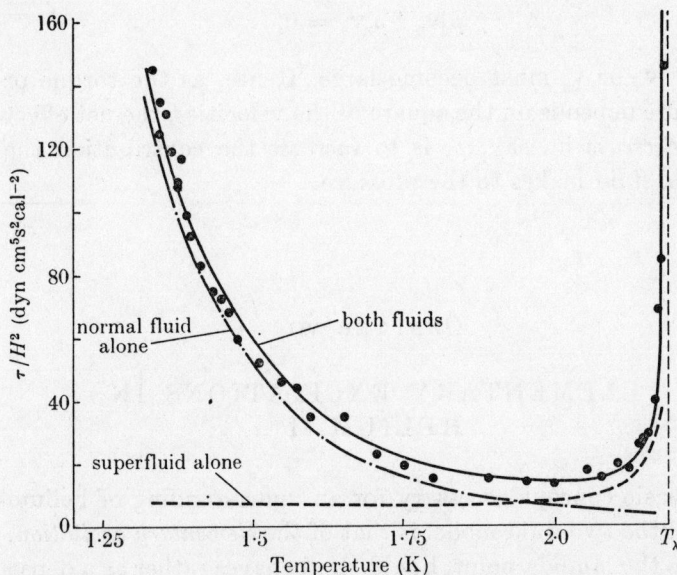

FIG. 6.4. The torque τ on a Rayleigh disc due to a heat flux H, plotted as τ/H^2 versus temperature. The points are experimentally determined; the lines show the theoretical contribution from the normal and superfluid, and from both fluids together (Pellam and Hanson [35]).

where c_2 is the velocity of second sound, ρ and C the density and specific heat of helium, and T the absolute temperature. Equation (6.10) has been verified for a uniform flow of heat, and also by observing the torque due to an oscillating flux of second sound impinging on a disc suspended from a torsion fibre. Because the reaction pressure depends on the square of the heat flux, there is a net torque on the disc even in an oscillating field, just as on a Rayleigh disc in the path of an ordinary sound wave.

The very characteristic temperature dependence of expression (6.10) is shown in Fig. 6.4, which also gives the contribution of each fluid to the total pressure. We see that the torque on a disc rises rapidly at both high and low temperatures. This comes about because either ρ_n or ρ_s is becoming very small. Hence in order to satisfy the condition for no net mass flow of helium

$$\rho_n v_n + \rho_n v_s = 0,$$

either v_n or v_s must become large. Hence, as the torque or pressure depends on the square of the velocities, the net effect of a *decrease* in, say, ρ_n is to *increase* the contribution the normal fluid makes to the pressure.

CHAPTER VII

ELEMENTARY EXCITATIONS IN HELIUM II

THE basic concept necessary for an understanding of helium II and the two-fluid model is that of the *elementary excitation*. Above the lambda point, liquid ^{4}He behaves rather as a dense classical gas, but at lower temperatures its behaviour is quite different. This is by no means surprising, as the de Broglie wavelengths of the helium atoms are comparable with the interatomic spacings. Therefore, as was first pointed out by Landau [33], it is necessary to describe the atomic motion in terms of elementary excitations.

We have already introduced the concept of elementary excitations when discussing the properties of liquid ^{3}He. We recall that in the Landau theory of a Fermi liquid the atoms were replaced by quasi-particles or elementary excitations. The dispersion relation for these excitations was a form of the single-particle relation $\epsilon = p^2/2m$, modified to take account of the interactions between the atoms. At first sight we might expect the excitations in ^{4}He to be rather similar, but the experiments we now describe show that the excitation spectrum is quite different. In fact, the properties of helium II below 0·6 K imply that the only thermal motion consists of phonons similar to those in crystalline solids. It will therefore be useful to summarize some well-known properties of phonons in such solids.

7.1. Phonons in crystalline solids

The standard treatment of the thermal vibrations of the atoms in crystalline solids is to resolve their motion into normal modes, which are plane waves occupying the whole volume of the solid. On quantizing these normal modes, and taking account of the periodicity of the lattice, we find that the energy of a quantum, or *phonon*, is related to its wave number by a relation $\epsilon = \epsilon(\mathbf{k})$ known as the energy spectrum or dispersion curve.

The form of the dispersion curve may be determined experimentally by observing the inelastic scattering of slow neutrons. The scattered neutrons have, in general, exchanged one quantum of energy with the vibrations of the lattice, and an analysis of their energies and momenta lead to the form of the energy spectrum. A typical result is shown in Fig. 7.1.

Given the form of the dispersion curve, we can deduce all the thermodynamic properties of the lattice using statistical mechanics, provided that the phonons are in a state of thermal equilibrium. In fact, this equilibrium is assured by the small anharmonic terms in the equations of motion of the atoms, which induce transitions between the normal modes. These transitions, besides establishing equilibrium, may also set a limit to the usefulness of our representation of thermal motion in terms of excitations. Thus, if the mean time between transitions is Δt, the energy of a state E is only sharp to within an energy ΔE given by the uncertainty principle

$$\Delta E \Delta t \sim \hbar.$$

Clearly, if an excitation is to be a meaningful concept, then ΔE must be considerably less than the energy E. However, this condition is generally well satisfied for phonons in solids.

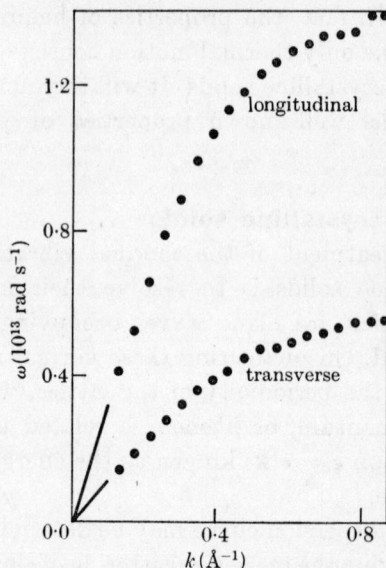

FIG. 7.1. The dispersion curve for transverse and longitudinal waves of wave number k and circular frequency ω in lead at 80 K (Stedman, Almquist, Nilsson, and Raunio [36]).

We are often concerned with non-equilibrium steady-state conditions, as for example in the flow of heat down a steady temperature gradient. We then need to specify how the state of the system is different at different points in space. The phonons so far described are plane waves occupying the whole volume of a solid, and therefore do not readily take account of spatial variations. We deal with such problems by making up localized excitations from wave packets of plane waves, which travel through the solid with the group velocity of the waves. A flow of heat between the hot and cold ends of a rod arises because the density of phonons is greater at the hotter end, and hence there is a larger flow of phonons towards the cold end than away from it.

The above picture of heat flow leads to the well-known expression for the thermal conductivity of a dielectric solid

$$K = \tfrac{1}{3}\mathscr{C}v\lambda,$$

where $\mathscr{C}$ is the specific heat per unit volume, v the velocity of sound, and λ the mean free path of the phonons between scattering processes. The conductivity is proportional to the rate of change of the phonon energy with temperature, and to the phonon velocity; that is to the specific heat and the velocity of sound. The mean free path takes account of the various scattering processes which impede the free flow of the phonons. In a pure dielectric material at room temperature the only scattering processes are between the phonons themselves, that is each phonon is scattered by the density variations due to other phonons.

Phonons interact with each other mainly by three-phonon processes of two types. *Normal processes* conserve energy and wave-vector, so that

$$\epsilon_1 + \epsilon_2 = \epsilon_3 \quad \text{and} \quad \mathbf{k}_1 + \mathbf{k}_2 = \mathbf{k}_3$$

and the flow of energy remains unchanged. On the other hand, *umklapp processes* do not conserve wave-vector; hence they scatter the phonons and produce a thermal resistance. The numbers of both types of interaction decrease rapidly with falling temperatures, so that eventually the mean free path is limited by the walls of the specimen, and the apparent conductivity is then proportional to the diameter of the specimen. This is the so-called size effect associated with boundary scattering.

7.2. Phonons in helium II

Below 0.6 K, the specific heat of liquid ^{4}He varies at T^3. This behaviour is quite different from that of a perfect gas of Bose particles with an energy spectrum $\epsilon = p^2/2m$, which would have a specific heat proportional to $T^{\frac{3}{2}}$ (see for example reference [37]). Moreover, the magnitude of the specific heat of liquid ^{4}He is almost exactly that given by Debye's theory for the specific heat of a *crystalline solid*, provided that we take only longitudinal modes into account, as the liquid cannot support shear waves. Thus, substituting the measured velocity of sound into the usual Debye formula,

we obtain

$$C_V = 0.0207 \times T^3 \text{ J g}^{-1} \text{ K}^{-1},$$

which is the same as the measured value, to within the experimental error of 2 per cent.

It is remarkable that the specific heat of any liquid may be calculated by assuming that the atomic motion is no more complex than in a solid. Nevertheless the assumption is supported by the form of the melting curve. As discussed in section 1.2, the vanishing of dP/dT implies that the entropy of the liquid along the melting curve is very close to that of the solid. In addition, the thermal conductivity of helium II below 0·6 K strongly suggests that the thermal motion may be completely described in terms of phonons.

Fig. 7.2 shows the thermal conductivity of the liquid, measured in two capillaries of diameter 0·29 and 0·80 mm. Below 0·6 K, the apparent conductivity varies as T^3, and is proportional to the diameter of the capillary. This behaviour is reminiscent of the heat flow in a dielectric crystal which is limited by boundary scattering. In fact the results of Fig. 7.2

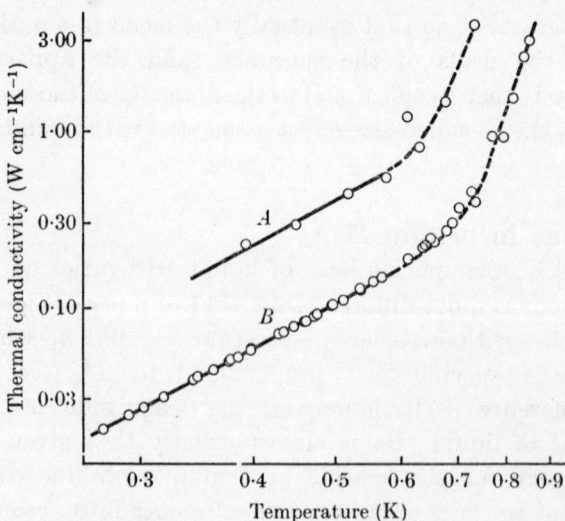

FIG. 7.2. The thermal conductivity of liquid ^{4}He: A, in a tube 0·80 mm diameter; B, in a tube 0·29 mm diameter (Fairbank and Wilks [38]).

may be represented by the usual formula for boundary scattering

$$K \simeq \tfrac{1}{3}\mathscr{C}vd,$$

where $\mathscr{C}$ is the specific heat per unit volume, v the velocity of sound, and d the diameter of the specimen.

To sum up, both the specific heat and thermal conductivity of helium II below 0·6 K suggest that the only modes of heat motion are longitudinal phonons analogous to those in a solid. Above 0·6 K the specific heat varies approximately as T^6, and rapidly increases above the Debye value, which implies that other modes of motion are being excited. The nature of these other modes, and the reason why they are not excited at lower temperatures, form one of the central problems of liquid helium II.

7.3. The scattering of neutrons by helium II

The possibility of detecting the thermal excitations in liquid helium II was first pointed out by Feynman and Cohen [39]. If a beam of monochromatic slow neutrons passes through a specimen of liquid helium, some neutrons will be scattered out of the beam, and the only scattering processes at all probable are ones in which the neutron creates or annihilates a single thermal excitation. Moreover, as the excitations obey Bose statistics, the probability of annihilating an excitation is proportional to $n(\epsilon) = (\exp(\epsilon/k_B T) - 1)^{-1}$, and the probability of creating an excitation to $n(\epsilon) + 1$. Hence as ϵ/k_B turns out to have a value of about 9 K, the creation process is much the more important.

Let us suppose that a beam of monochromatic neutrons of wave number $\mathbf{q}_i$ is incident on a sample of liquid and that the scattered neutrons have a range of wave numbers $\mathbf{q}_s$. We also suppose that each neutron creates an excitation of wave number $\mathbf{k}$ which has an energy

$$\epsilon = \epsilon(k),$$

where $\epsilon(k)$ is some unique relation to be determined. Note that ϵ depends only on k, the modulus of $\mathbf{k}$, as the liquid is isotropic.

Applying the conservation of energy to one scattering process,

$$\frac{\hbar^2}{2m}(q_i^2 - q_s^2) = \epsilon(k);$$

also, the strength of the scattered beam vanishes unless

$$\mathbf{q}_i - \mathbf{q}_s = \mathbf{k}.$$

Hence by measuring $\mathbf{q}_i$ and $\mathbf{q}_s$ we obtain one pair of values of ϵ and $\mathbf{k}$ corresponding to one particular excitation in the liquid.

If we perform a neutron scattering experiment on an ordinary liquid using a monochromatic incident beam, then the neutrons scattered in one given direction exhibit a wide range of energies. However, in helium II the heat motion is much reduced, and it is found that neutrons scattered in a given direction have almost the same energy value. We thus obtain sets of values of ϵ and k for the elementary excitations, which we use to trace out the dispersion curve. (The scattered neutrons do not have exactly the same energy, as the thermal excitations interact with each other. Hence, they have a finite lifetime τ, and an energy uncertainty given by the uncertainty principle $\Delta\epsilon \sim \hbar/\tau$. This effect is small below 1 K, but becomes more marked towards the lambda point. Eventually, above the lambda point, the scattered neutrons have the wide spread of energy characteristic of an ordinary liquid.)

Fig. 7.3 shows the dispersion curve for the excitations in helium II obtained by neutron scattering, the momenta being given in units of wave number. Note that the dispersion curve does not end abruptly at a wave number of about 2.8 Å^{-1}, as is suggested by the figure. In this region the curve becomes difficult to measure, because the cross-section corresponding to the creation of single excitations falls off rapidly with increasing wave number. For small wave numbers the curve is linear, with a slope closely related to the velocity of sound, the excitations in this region are phonons specified by the relation

$$\epsilon = c\hbar k. \tag{7.1}$$

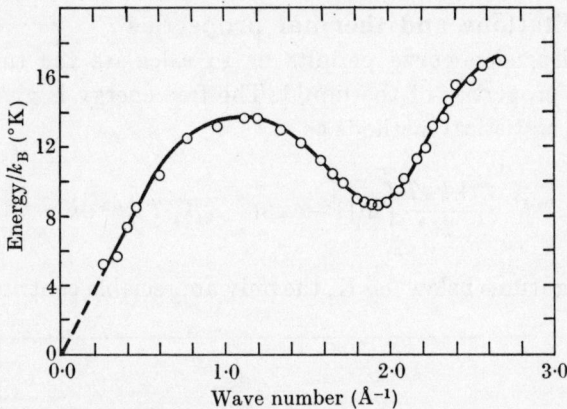

Fɪɢ. 7.3. The dispersion curve for thermal excitations in liquid He II at 1·12 K, as deduced from the neutron scattering experiments (Henshaw and Woods [40]).

We discuss the nature of the excitations of higher momenta in Chapter 11. (It would be interesting to make similar measurements on liquid ^{3}He to verify the energy spectrum of section 3.2, but this is almost impossible as the ^{3}He nucleus has a very large cross-section for the capture of thermal neutrons.)

Finally we note one important difference between phonons in liquid helium and phonons in a solid. For phonons and other excitations in helium II we will make use of the standard wave-mechanical relation between wave-vector and momentum, namely $\mathbf{p} = \hbar \mathbf{k}$. However, the normal modes of a crystal lattice are set up by resolving the atomic motions into purely vibrational states plus a translational motion *which is the same for all the atoms*. Hence any momentum of the crystal is associated only with the translation motion, and not with the vibrational modes or phonons. In this case, the quantity $\hbar \mathbf{k}$ is not a momentum, although it is sometimes termed a 'quasi-momentum'. In a liquid, the position is quite different. Thus in neutron scattering experiments with a crystal, the lattice is fixed to the spectrometer table, which takes up the recoil of the scattered neutron. A liquid has no rigid lattice, so the recoil momentum is taken up by the individual excitations which have a real momentum $\mathbf{p} = \hbar \mathbf{k}$.

7.4. Excitations and thermal properties

The dispersion curve permits us to calculate the thermo-dynamic properties of the liquid. The free energy is given by standard statistical methods as

$$F = \frac{Vk_BT}{2\pi^2}\int\limits_0^\infty \ln\{1-\exp(-\epsilon_k/k_BT)\}k^2\,dk. \qquad (7.2)$$

At temperatures below 0·5 K, the only appreciable contribution

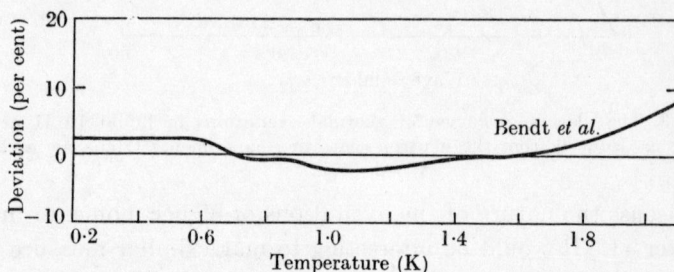

Fig. 7.4. The full line shows the percentage deviation between values of the entropy calculated by Bendt, Cowan, and Yarnell [41] and values determined experimentally.

comes from the linear part of the spectrum, and the specific heat

$$C_{\mathrm{ph}} = \frac{2\pi^2k_B^4}{15\rho\hbar^3c^3}T^3,$$

which is the usual Debye expression for a continuum.

Above 0·5 or 0·6 K excitations of higher momentum are excited. In this case, the thermodynamic functions have to be evaluated by numerical computation. There is also the complica-tion that the form of the dispersion curve depends slightly on the temperature, but we do not pursue this point further. Fig. 7.4 shows the good agreement of the entropy calculated via equation (7.2) with values determined from the measured specific heat, at least to temperatures of about 1·8 K. (At higher temperatures, the number of excitations becomes so large that the interactions between them must be taken into account.)

7.5. Phonons and rotons

When calculating the entropy, Bendt *et al.* divided their dispersion curve into four momentum regions for ease of computation, as shown in Fig. 7.5. (In the fourth momentum interval they assumed that the slope of the curve finally becomes equal to the velocity of sound. Such behaviour is not consistent with later experiments, but the contribution of these levels to the thermodynamic functions is small.) Fig. 7.6 shows how excitations of different momenta contribute to the total entropy. At the lowest temperatures all the excitations are phonons corresponding to the initial linear part of the dispersion curve. As the temperature is raised, excitations in the region of the minimum are created and cause the entropy to rise rapidly above the Debye value. At all temperatures, the entropy arises principally from excitations in one or both of the momentum intervals 1 and 3, although at the higher

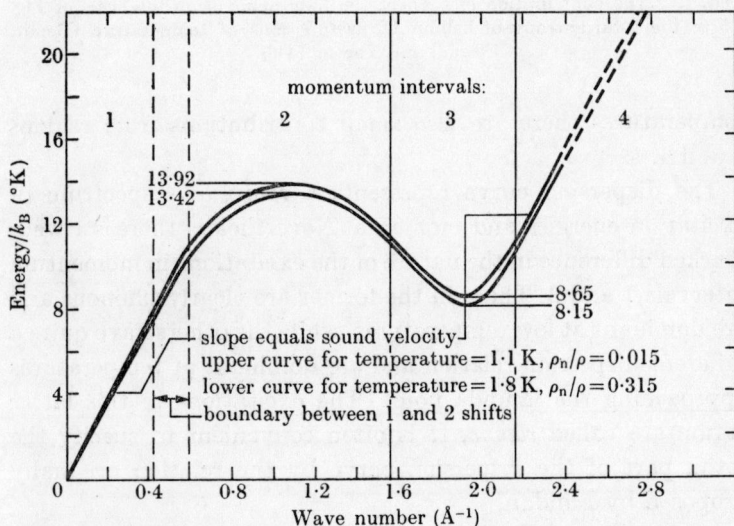

FIG. 7.5. The excitation curve at $1 \cdot 1$ and $1 \cdot 8$ K divided into four momentum intervals (Bendt, Cowan, and Yarnell [41]). (The position of the boundary between intervals 1 and 2 depends slightly on the temperature. Note that the form of the extrapolated curves in region 4 differs from the experimental results of reference [40] shown in Fig. 7.3.)

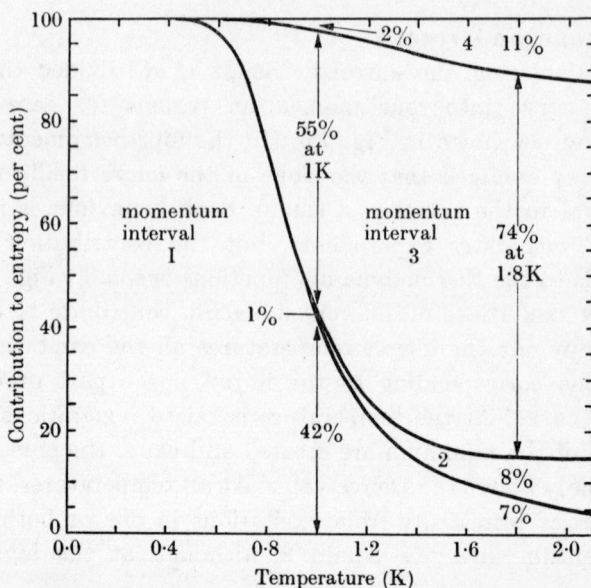

FIG. 7.6. The contribution of each of the four momentum intervals of Fig. 7.5 to the total entropy of helium II, as functions of temperature (Bendt, Cowan, and Yarnell [41]).

temperatures there are also small contributions from regions 2 and 4.

The dispersion curve represents a *continuous* spectrum of excitation energies and momenta. Nevertheless there is a well-marked difference in the nature of the excitations in momentum intervals 1 and 3. Those in the former are clearly phonons and are dominant at low temperatures, while the others have quite a different dispersion relation and are dominant at temperatures approaching the lambda point. The excitations in this latter region are called *rotons*. It is often convenient to specify the roton part of the dispersion curve by the relation originally proposed by Landau,

$$\epsilon = \Delta + \frac{(p - p_0)^2}{2\mu}, \tag{7.3}$$

where Δ and p_0 are the energy and momentum coordinates of the minimum and μ is a constant related to the curvature at the minimum, with values

$$\Delta/k_B \sim 8{\cdot}65 \pm 0{\cdot}04 \text{ K}$$
$$p_0/\hbar \sim 1{\cdot}91 \pm 0{\cdot}01 \text{ Å}^{-1} \qquad (7.4)$$
$$\mu \sim (0{\cdot}16)m_4,$$

k_B being Boltzmann's constant, and m_4 the mass of a ^{4}He atom. We discuss the nature of the roton excitations in Chapter 11, but note here that any similarity between the words roton and rotation must be treated very cautiously.

By substituting (7.3) into equation (7.2) we obtain the contribution of the rotons to the thermodynamic functions. For example the roton entropy

$$S_r = \frac{2(k_B\mu)^{\frac{1}{2}}p_0^2\Delta}{(2\pi)^{\frac{3}{2}}\rho\hbar^3 T^{\frac{1}{2}}}\left(1+\frac{3k_B T}{2\Delta}\right)e^{-\Delta/k_B T}. \qquad (7.5)$$

It follows that the constants Δ, p_0, and μ may be deduced from the properties of helium II without reference to the neutron scattering experiments. Thus Δ may be determined by an analysis of the temperature dependence of the entropy. At temperatures below about $1{\cdot}3$ K the excitations lie mostly in the phonon or roton parts of the spectrum. In this case the roton contribution to the entropy S_r is closely equal to $(S-S_{ph})$ where S is the total measured entropy, and S_{ph} the phonon entropy. By plotting these values of S_r against the temperature in the form of equation (7.5), one obtains a value for Δ in agreement with (7.4). Finally, by measuring ρ_n, the density of the normal fluid, we may combine equation (7.5) and equations (8.10) of the next chapter to obtain the values of p_0 and μ.

CHAPTER VIII

THE THEORETICAL BASIS OF THE TWO-FLUID MODEL

WE now show how the two-fluid model may be deduced from the properties of the elementary thermal excitations. We begin by giving Landau's discussion of superfluidity and the density of the normal fluid.

8.1. Superfluidity

To maintain the flow of an ordinary liquid through a capillary, it is necessary to apply a pressure, and most of the work done by this pressure appears as heat in the liquid. Without going into any details of the viscous processes, we can say that the resistance to flow arises because of a conversion of some of the kinetic energy of the liquid into disordered thermal motion. Or, put another way, the relative motion of liquid and capillary sets up additional thermal motion in the liquid, and this is the source of the viscous reaction. We now show that excitations can only be formed in helium II, as the result of flow past a wall, if the helium has a certain minimum velocity. If this velocity is not exceeded, there is no energy dissipation arising from the flow, and no viscous loss.

Consider a mass of liquid helium at absolute zero passing through a tube or capillary with streamline flow. How will it respond to the reactions of the wall which tend to slow it down? If the helium were a solid it could slow down by reducing its overall velocity, but this is not physically sensible for a liquid. The slowing down process can only be brought about by the gradual excitation of internal motions in the liquid in the layers close to the wall.

Let us suppose that helium is flowing through a tube which is so constrained that it may move freely in the direction of its length but in no other direction. We regard the flow through the tube from a coordinate system in which the helium is at rest, and the tube moving with velocity v. Let us further suppose that the relative motion of tube and liquid creates an excitation in the liquid with energy ϵ and momentum $\mathbf{p}$. If the tube and the helium form an isolated system, then the tube will lose an amount of energy

$$\Delta E = \epsilon. \qquad (8.1)$$

The tube will also lose momentum $\Delta \mathbf{P}$ directed along its length, and from the conservation of momentum it follows that

$$|\Delta \mathbf{P}| \leqslant p, \tag{8.2}$$

the equality sign being valid if the excitation moves parallel to the length of the tube. The velocity of the tube will be reduced by an amount $\Delta \mathbf{P}/M$, where M is its mass. Hence provided that the momentum of the tube Mv is much greater than that of the excitation, as will be the case, it is a good approximation to write

$$\Delta E = v\,|\Delta \mathbf{P}|. \tag{8.3}$$

Combining (8.1), (8.2), and (8.3) we obtain

$$v > \epsilon/p. \tag{8.4}$$

That is, an excitation can only be created as the result of the flow if the velocity is at least ϵ/p.

Landau's relation (8.4) shows that a certain minimum velocity of flow v_c is needed to create an excitation in the moving helium. In the initial linear phonon region of the spectrum $\epsilon = cp$ so that v_c is equal to the velocity of sound ($\sim 2 \times 10^4$ cm s^{-1}). The minimum value of ϵ/p for any excitation is seen by inspection of the dispersion curve (Fig. 7.3) to occur in the region of the minimum (roton excitations) and to be approximately equal to Δ/p_0 (6×10^3 cm s^{-1}). Hence, provided no other internal motions are possible, superfluidity should persist up to these high velocities.

Landau's argument explains in principle why helium II is superfluid, but does not lead to the correct values for the critical velocity. The observed critical velocities are much lower than the 60 m s^{-1} predicted for the creation of rotons, being generally of the order of a few cm s^{-1} or less. This discrepancy comes about because Landau assumes that the flow of the liquid is streamline, and thus rules out the possibility of other forms of internal motion besides the phonons and rotons. In fact we describe in Chapters 13 and 14 experiments which show that vortex-like motions are set up by relatively low velocities of flow. We defer until that chapter all discussion as to the value of the relevant critical velocity.

Although Landau did not predict the correct value of the critical velocity, his discussion of the creation of thermal excitations is *essential* to explain why the liquid is superfluid. To appreciate this point, let us consider the flow of an ordinary liquid through a tube. In this case, the thermal excitations are excitations of single atoms, and the dispersion curve has the form $\epsilon = p^2/2m$. Thus, for sufficiently small values of p, there will always be possible excitations for which ϵ/p is less than any specified velocity. Therefore excitations can always be created by flow, and the liquid is not a superfluid. The superfluidity of helium II arises from the difficulty of creating the particular forms of thermal excitations which are permitted in the liquid.

8.2. The Galilean transformation

Before proceeding further, we collect here one or two riders concerning the Galilean transformation between two co-ordinate systems with relative velocity v, as shown in Fig. 8.1. The relation between the two sets of coordinates is

$$\mathbf{r}' = \mathbf{r} + \mathbf{v}t \qquad \text{and} \qquad t' = t.$$

It follows directly from classical mechanics that the energies (E', E) and momenta $(\mathbf{P}', \mathbf{P})$ of a body of mass M as viewed from the two systems are related by the equations

$$E' = E + \mathbf{P} \cdot \mathbf{v} + \tfrac{1}{2}Mv^2,$$

$$\mathbf{P}' = \mathbf{P} + M\mathbf{v}.$$

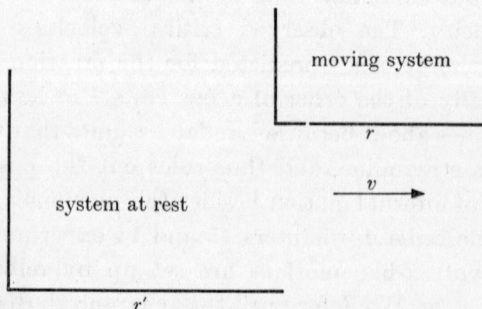

FIG. 8.1. Two coordinate systems with relative velocity v; see text.

We will need expressions relating the energies and momenta of an excitation viewed from these two coordinate systems. We therefore consider a mass M of helium at temperature zero, containing no excitations, moving with velocity $\mathbf{v}$ relative to the laboratory coordinates. To an observer moving with the liquid, the helium has zero momentum and an energy E_0. To an observer at rest in the laboratory, the helium will have a

TABLE 8.1

	Momentum		Energy	
	Coordinate system moving with the helium	Laboratory coordinate system	Coordinate system moving with the helium	Laboratory coordinate system
No excitations present	0	$M\mathbf{v}$	E_0	$E_0 + \frac{1}{2}Mv^2$
One excitation present	$\mathbf{p}$	$\mathbf{p} + M\mathbf{v}$	$E_0 + \epsilon$	$E_0 + \epsilon + \frac{1}{2}Mv^2 + \mathbf{p} \cdot \mathbf{v}$

momentum and energy given by the above transformations, namely $M\mathbf{v}$ and $E_0 + \frac{1}{2}Mv^2$ as set out in Table 8.1. Let us now suppose that an excitation is created in the liquid, so that the observer moving with the liquid sees a total momentum $\mathbf{p}$ and a total energy $E_0 + \epsilon$. The total momentum and energy as seen by the laboratory observer are again given by the Galilean transformation, and are $\mathbf{p} + M\mathbf{v}$ and $E_0 + \epsilon + \frac{1}{2}Mv^2 + \mathbf{p} \cdot \mathbf{v}$ respectively. These results are displayed in Table 8.1. We see that, as far as the laboratory observer is concerned, the extra momentum and energy associated with the excitation are $\mathbf{p}$ and $\epsilon + \mathbf{p} \cdot \mathbf{v}$. Hence the relation between the energy appropriate to the moving coordinate system and to the laboratory system (indicated by primes) is

$$\epsilon' = \epsilon + \mathbf{p} \cdot \mathbf{v}. \tag{8.5}$$

We also see that the momentum (or wave number) is invariant to the relative velocity of two systems, that is

$$\mathbf{p}' = \mathbf{p}. \tag{8.6}$$

We now consider how the distribution function must be modified when the excitations have an imposed drift velocity $\mathbf{v}_n$ relative to the observer. To fix our ideas, let us commence with the helium at rest, in equilibrium, and in the same coordinate system as the observer. The appropriate distribution function is the usual expression for an unspecified number of Bose particles

$$n_0(\epsilon) = \{\exp(\epsilon/k_B T) - 1\}^{-1}. \tag{8.7}$$

We then impose a drift velocity $\mathbf{v}_n$ on the excitations. For an observer moving with this velocity the distribution is still given by (8.7). That is, he sees a certain number, $n_0(\epsilon)$, of excitations with energy ϵ. However, to a stationary observer these excitations appear to have an energy $\epsilon + \mathbf{p} \cdot \mathbf{v}_n$, in accord with equation (8.5). Hence for an observer at rest

$$n_0(\epsilon + \mathbf{p} \cdot \mathbf{v}_n) = \{\exp \epsilon(p)/k_B T - 1\}^{-1}$$

or, what amounts to the same thing,

$$n_0(\epsilon) = \{\exp(\epsilon - \mathbf{p} \cdot \mathbf{v}_n)/k_B T - 1\}^{-1}. \tag{8.8}$$

8.3. The normal density

The frictionless flow of helium II at absolute zero comes about because of the difficulty of creating excitations mechanically. We now consider the behaviour of the liquid when it flows through a capillary at higher temperatures, when some thermal excitations are already present. The argument used to derive the critical velocity did not depend on the fact that the helium was in its ground state. Hence no new excitations will be produced by flow at higher temperatures unless the same critical velocities are exceeded. However, the existing excitations will collide with the walls of the tube, and momentum will be exchanged between the tube and the liquid.

Consider a mass of helium II in a long, straight tube of negligible thermal capacity, both the tube and the helium being at rest and at temperature zero. The temperature of the helium is then raised so as to create excitations thermally. These excitations have energies and momenta, ϵ and $\mathbf{p}$, which are the quantities measured in neutron scattering experiments. The tube is next moved relative to the helium in a direction along its length. Because of collisions with the tube, the excitations will eventually come into equilibrium with a drift velocity equal to that of the tube, say $\mathbf{v_n}$.

Let us now calculate the total momentum associated with the excitations in a volume V of liquid helium. By symmetry, the net momentum of the excitations $\mathbf{P}$ must be in a direction parallel or anti-parallel to $\mathbf{v_n}$. Also, the density of states in p space is $4\pi V p^2 \, \mathrm{d}p/h^3$, and of these states a fraction $\frac{1}{2} \sin \theta \, \mathrm{d}\theta$ corresponds to values of $\mathbf{p}$ making angles with $\mathbf{v_n}$ in the range θ to $\theta + \mathrm{d}\theta$. Hence the net momentum of the excitations is

$$\mathbf{P} = \int\limits_{0}^{\infty}\int\limits_{0}^{\pi} p \cos \theta \, . \, n' \, . \, \frac{4\pi V p^2}{h^3} \, \mathrm{d}p \, . \, \tfrac{1}{2} \sin \theta \, \mathrm{d}\theta,$$

where n' is the actual (non-equilibrium) value of the distribution function. Expanding n' about its equilibrium value in powers of $\mathbf{v_n}$, neglecting second order and higher terms, and integrating over θ, we obtain

$$\mathbf{P} = \rho_\mathrm{n} V \mathbf{v_n} ,$$

where

$$\rho_\mathrm{n} = -\frac{4\pi}{3h^3} \int \frac{\partial}{\partial \epsilon} \{\exp \epsilon/k_\mathrm{B}T - 1\}^{-1} p^4 \, \mathrm{d}p. \qquad (8.9)$$

Note that ρ_n is an essentially positive quantity with the dimensions of density, and is a function of temperature, but not of $\mathbf{v_n}$.

Values of ρ_n derived from equation (8.9) and the dispersion relation given by the neutron scattering experiments are shown by the full line in Fig. 8.2. Note that ρ_n approaches the total density ρ at the lambda point, and becomes very small at low

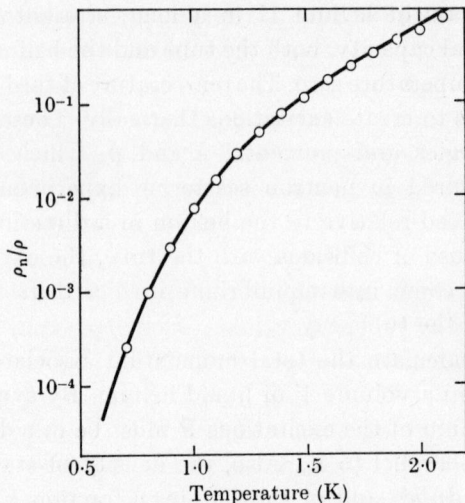

FIG. 8.2. The full line shows values of ρ_n/ρ derived from neutron scattering experiments by Bendt, Cowan, and Yarnell [41]. The points indicate values derived from the velocity of second sound.

temperatures. By substituting into (8.9) the dispersion relations for the phonon and roton parts of the excitation spectrum, we find that the phonon and roton contributions to ρ_n are

$$\rho_{\mathrm{nph}} = \frac{2\pi^2 k_{\mathrm{B}}^4}{45\hbar^3 c^5} T^4,$$

$$\rho_{\mathrm{nr}} = \frac{2\mu^{\frac{1}{2}} p_0^4}{3(2\pi)^{\frac{3}{2}}(k_{\mathrm{B}} T)^{\frac{1}{2}}\hbar^3} e^{-\Delta/k_{\mathrm{B}}T}. \tag{8.10}$$

The two contributions are equal at about 0.5 K, but ρ_{nph} increases much less rapidly with rising temperature than ρ_{nr}, and therefore contributes less than 1 per cent of the total value above about 1.2 K.

If the helium were an ordinary liquid it would eventually come into equilibrium with the moving tube and have a momentum $\rho V \mathbf{v}_{\mathrm{n}}$. In fact the only momentum transfer is to the excitations, and the above argument shows that the equilibrium momentum is $\rho_{\mathrm{n}} V \mathbf{v}_{\mathrm{n}}$, where $\rho_{\mathrm{n}} \leqslant \rho$. Therefore the reaction of the liquid on the tube is less than for a normal liquid, and as far as the tube is concerned the helium appears to have a density of only ρ_n. This is the type of situation encountered in Andronikashvili's experiment (section 6.5) and we therefore identify ρ_n with the density of the normal fluid in the two-fluid model. We see from Fig. 8.2 that the calculated values are in good agreement with those derived from experiments on second sound.

8.4. The two-fluid model

We now generalize the argument of the previous section. Suppose that liquid helium at temperature zero is contained in a tube, and that both helium and tube are moving relative to the observer in the laboratory with a velocity $\mathbf{v}_s$. The temperature is then raised so as to create excitations. The energy and momentum of an excitation as seen by an observer travelling with the liquid are ϵ and $\mathbf{p}$, related by the dispersion curve of Fig. 7.3; but to an observer in the laboratory these quantities appear to have values

$$\epsilon' = \epsilon + \mathbf{p} \cdot \mathbf{v}_s \qquad \mathbf{p}' = \mathbf{p} \qquad (8.11)$$

in accord with the transformations (8.5) and (8.6). The tube is now given a steady velocity relative to the laboratory of $\mathbf{v}_n$ so that when equilibrium is reached the *excitations* have a drift velocity of $\mathbf{v}_n$. The appropriate distribution function for the excitations as viewed by a laboratory observer is now given by a generalization of equation (8.8), namely

$$n'(\mathbf{p}) = [\exp\{(\overline{\epsilon + \mathbf{p} \cdot \mathbf{v}_s} - \mathbf{p} \cdot \mathbf{v}_n)/k_B T\} - 1]^{-1}$$
$$= [\exp\{(\epsilon - \mathbf{p} \cdot \overline{\mathbf{v}_n - \mathbf{v}_s})/k_B T\} - 1]^{-1}. \qquad (8.12)$$

This expression is similar to (8.8), save that $\mathbf{v}_n$ is replaced by $\mathbf{v}_n - \mathbf{v}_s$. Hence we may proceed as in the previous section, and find that the net momentum of the excitations is now

$$\mathbf{P} = \rho_n(\mathbf{v}_n - \mathbf{v}_s)V,$$

where ρ_n is defined as previously. The total momentum of the liquid as viewed by the laboratory observer before the creation of the excitations was $\rho V \mathbf{v}_s$. Therefore the total momentum per unit volume when the excitations are present is

$$\mathbf{j} = \rho\mathbf{v_s} + \rho_n(\mathbf{v_n} - \mathbf{v_s}). \tag{8.13}$$

We now define a new parameter ρ_s by the relation

$$\rho = \rho_n + \rho_s, \tag{8.14}$$

and then rewrite equation (8.13) as

$$\mathbf{j} = \rho_n\mathbf{v_n} + \rho_s\mathbf{v_s}. \tag{8.15}$$

The momentum of the system is now formally resolved into the two components of the two-fluid model.

To complete our derivation of the two-fluid model, we consider the total rate of change of the energy and momentum of the excitations in a unit volume fixed in the laboratory system of coordinates. Changes in this energy and momentum arise

(i) by a change in the number of excitations as the result of flow through the boundaries of the volume,

(ii) by a change in the energy and momentum of the excitations originally present, arising from changes in the density of the helium ρ and from changes in the velocity $\mathbf{v_s}$.

Hence, by writing down equations for the energy and momentum balance, we obtain the entropy conservation equation

$$\frac{\partial(\rho S)}{\partial t} = -\mathrm{div}(\rho S\mathbf{v_n}) \tag{6.5}$$

and

$$\rho_n\frac{\partial}{\partial t}(\mathbf{v_n} - \mathbf{v_s}) = -\rho S\ \mathrm{grad}\ T,$$

which is equivalent to equation (6.6) of the two-fluid model (after substituting for grad P from (6.4)).

Finally, as a check to see that our method of calculation is physically meaningful we now calculate ρ_n for a perfect gas obeying Boltzmann statistics. Replacing (8.7) by the Boltzmann distribution, and proceeding as before, we find that $\rho_n = \rho$, the total density, as we would expect. Similarly $\rho_n = \rho$ for a perfect gas obeying Fermi statistics, and for a perfect gas obeying Bose statistics at temperatures above the condensation temperature. However, for a perfect Bose gas below the condensation temperature, $\rho_n = \rho(N_c/N)$ where (N_c/N) is the fraction of molecules in the condensed state.

The last result clearly suggests that Bose statistics are very relevant to the existence of the two-fluid model. Yet liquid helium is certainly not a perfect gas. The transition temperature in the liquid is depressed as the pressure is increased, whereas in a perfect gas the condensation temperature rises. The specific heat of a Bose gas varies as $T^{\frac{3}{2}}$ at the lowest temperatures, whereas liquid helium has a specific heat varying as T^3. We return to this point in chapter 15.

8.5. Second sound

In this section we consider a relatively simple interpretation of the propagation of second sound or temperature waves. The simplest case occurs when the only excitations are phonons. The Boltzmann equation for the phonon distribution function $n(x_i, p_i)$ may then be written, using tensor notation, as

$$\frac{\partial n}{\partial t} + \frac{cp_i}{p}\frac{\partial n}{\partial x_i} = I_n \qquad (p = |p_i|),$$

where we assume that all the phonons travel with the same velocity c, and I_n is the rate of change of n due to collisions. Assuming conservation of energy and momentum in the collisions, it follows that

$$\frac{\partial E}{\partial t} + c^2\frac{\partial P_i}{\partial x_i} = 0 \qquad \text{and} \qquad \frac{\partial P_i}{\partial t} + c\frac{\partial T_{ik}}{\partial x_k} = 0,$$

where

$$E = \int ncp\, \mathrm{d}^3p \qquad P_i = \int np_i\, \mathrm{d}^3p \qquad T_{ik} = \int \frac{p_i p_k}{p}n\, \mathrm{d}^3p.$$

Assuming also that the distribution function is disturbed only slightly from spherical symmetry, $T_{ik} \simeq \frac{1}{3}\delta_{ik}E/c$ so that

$$\frac{\partial^2 E}{\partial t^2} = \frac{c^2}{3}\frac{\partial^2 E}{\partial x_i^2}. \tag{8.16}$$

As E is proportional to the energy density, equation (8.16) is the equation of a temperature wave propagating with a velocity $c/\sqrt{3}$.

An extension of the above method for the more general case of excitations with a spectrum $\epsilon = f(p)$ leads to a wave velocity given by

$$c_2^2 = \frac{\rho TS^2}{\rho_n C},\qquad(8.17)$$

which differs from the usual two-fluid expression by a factor ρ_s/ρ. However, at temperatures below 1 K this factor is unity to within 1 per cent or less, so that (8.17) gives virtually the same velocity as the standard formula. In the low-temperature limit when only phonons are present (8.17) leads to the velocity $c_2 = c/\sqrt{3}$ predicted by (8.16). Thus at the lower temperatures we may picture second sound as a fluctuation in the distribution function, propagating as a harmonic wave in the gas of excitations. At higher temperatures the picture is more complicated because an appreciable mass of the liquid is associated with the excitations. (This is taken into account by the factor ρ_s/ρ.)

For this model of second sound to be valid, two conditions are essential. Firstly there must be sufficient interaction between the excitations, so that a local equilibrium can be established within distances which are small compared with the wavelength of the sound. That is, the mean free path of the excitations between collisions must be appreciably less than the wavelength of the sound. Estimates of the mean free path may be derived from the theory of the normal viscosity η_n, described in the next chapter. It turns out that above 1 K the mean free path is much smaller than the wavelength in any of the experiments so far reported. However, the mean free path increases rapidly with falling temperature because the number of excitations decreases. Hence at lower temperatures it eventually becomes difficult to obtain signals of second sound. Several authors have investigated the propagation of second sound below 1 K using the pulse method; as the temperature is lowered, the pulse travels faster through the liquid in accord with the two-fluid expression of section 6.3, but its shape changes considerably. This effect is shown in Fig. 8.3, which is based on photographs of pulses displayed on an oscilloscope. At a temperature of 1·17 K the transmitted pulse is well defined, and characteristic of second sound. At 0·75 K the pulse has moved to the left, nearer to the start of the time base, and is appreciably wider; by 0·26 K the trace is so different that we cannot speak of a second-sound pulse at all.

The second condition for the propagation of second sound is that collisions between the excitations must conserve energy and momentum (or, more accurately, wave-vector). For

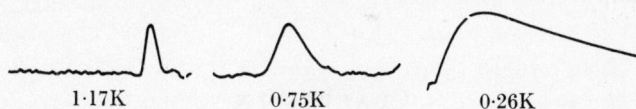

1·17K   0·75K   0·26K

FIG. 8.3. The shape of heat pulses transmitted through helium II at various temperatures as viewed on an oscilloscope trace; for details see text (after Kramers [42]).

example, if any umklapp-type collisions (cf. section 7.1) were to occur in helium II, second sound would only be possible if the mean free path between such collisions were much longer than the wavelength of the sound. In fact there are no umklapp processes in helium II, as the liquid has no regular lattice structure. Hence this second condition is always satisfied.

Finally we note that this treatment of second sound should apply to any substance in which the only excitations are phonons; hence we might expect to observe temperature waves in dielectric solids. From what we have said above, second sound will only be observed if

$$\lambda_N \ll l \ll \lambda_U , \qquad (8.18)$$

where λ_N and λ_U are the mean free paths between Normal collisions which conserve wave-vector, and between Umklapp collisions which do not, and where l is the wavelength of the sound. Equation (8.18) shows that to observe second sound we must select a crystal in which N processes are much more frequent than U processes. In principle this should be possible as the number of N processes varies as a power law of the temperature, whereas the number of U processes varies exponentially with temperature. Hence, by going to sufficiently low temperatures, λ_N will always be smaller than λ_U. However, in most crystals, the value of λ_N is then so large that the phonons are scattered diffusely by impurity atoms and by the walls of the specimen. However, recent experiments on the transmission of heat pulses in solid helium show that the second sound mode of propagation may be observed over a limited temperature range (see reference [43]). (The fact that solid *helium* has been the first solid to exhibit second sound appears quite coincidental.)

CHAPTER IX

KINETIC PROCESSES IN HELIUM II

WE described in Chapter 8 how the two-fluid model may be derived by regarding helium II as an assembly of elementary excitations. We now outline how this approach has been extended by Landau and Khalatnikov to account for the coefficient of the normal viscosity, for a coefficient analogous to the thermal conductivity of an ordinary liquid, and for the attenuation of sound and temperature waves.

The above coefficients are estimated by regarding the helium as an assembly of interacting excitations subject to a velocity or temperature gradient, or to an applied periodic disturbance. The calculations are then analogous to those used when computing the thermal conductivity of a dielectric solid. For example, the phonons in a solid diffuse under the influence of a temperature gradient, the actual rate of flow being determined by the number and nature of the collisions between them. The position in helium is similar, but more involved, as there is a larger spectrum of excitations, and several different types of possible collisions. As the calculations are somewhat lengthy, we shall only summarize the main results.

9.1. The normal viscosity

As mentioned in section 7.1, interactions between excitations will transfer a system from one state to another, giving a finite lifetime to each state. One such interaction involving a total of five excitations might be written schematically as

$$E_1 + E_2 + E_3 \rightleftharpoons E_4 + E_5.$$

We see that although energy is conserved, the number of excitations may or may not be. As in section 7.1, we regard the excitations as being localized, and talk of the interactions between them as collisions; this is a convenient representation though not a necessary one.

Collisions will occur between excitations of all wave numbers, and therefore the evaluation of the collision integral is very involved. To simplify the problem, Landau and Khalatnikov note that below about 1·5 K the excitations are predominantly those which can be represented by either the phonon or roton spectrum. They therefore confine their attention to phonons and rotons. The most probable types of collisions are in general those involving the smallest number of excitations. In fact the behaviour of the liquid can be accounted for by considering the following processes (not all of which are equally important):

3-phonon	$P_1 \rightleftharpoons P_2 + P_3$
3-roton	$R_1 \rightleftharpoons R_2 + R_3$
4-phonon	$P_1 + P_2 \rightleftharpoons P_3 + P_4$
4-roton	$R_1 + R_2 \rightleftharpoons R_3 + R_4$
5-phonon	$P_1 + P_2 \rightleftharpoons P_3 + P_4 + P_4$
P-R Scattering	$P_1 + R_1 \rightleftharpoons P_2 + R_2$
P-R Conversion	$P_1 + R_1 \rightleftharpoons R_2 + R_3$

By considering the above processes in detail, Landau and Khalatnikov obtain expressions for the various collision cross-sections. The phonon cross-sections depend principally on the velocity of sound and its variation with the density, while the roton cross-sections involve an interaction function which has to be determined from experiment as described below. It is then possible to write down a Boltzmann transport equation for the motion of the excitations, and to calculate the momentum flux when a velocity gradient is imposed on the system. The calculation is complicated as we must integrate over all possible values of the momenta of the excitations, and it is also necessary to

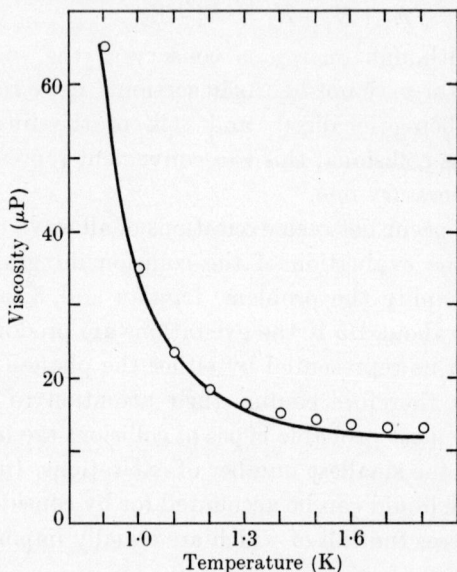

FIG. 9.1. Values of the normal viscosity η_n derived theoretically (Khalatnikov [44]). The points show experimental values.

decide which of the various collision processes are the most important.

It turns out that the normal viscosity η_n has two components η_r and η_{ph}. The first component η_r is associated with a flux of rotons scattered mainly by rotons. The number of rotons falls exponentially with temperature, but their mean free path increases at about the same rate, so this viscosity turns out to be independent of temperature. The component η_{ph} arises from a flux of phonons which is scattered principally by the rotons. As the liquid is cooled the number of phonons is reduced, nevertheless the viscosity rises because the number of rotons (causing scattering) decreases exponentially. Note that the value of η_r depends on the magnitude of the unknown interaction, but that η_{ph} is completely specified by the theory.

To compare these results with experiment, we restrict ourselves to values of the viscosity below about 1·9 K, because at temperatures near the lambda point the excitations are so numerous that interaction effects become important. Between about 1·5 and 1·9 K the viscosity does not change much with temperature, and the calculated value of η_{ph} is very small. Landau and Khalatnikov therefore identified the whole of the viscosity in this region with η_r, and wrote $\eta_r = 1·2 \times 10^{-5}$ poise. Then, calculating values of η_{ph}, they derived the total viscosity $(\eta_r + \eta_{ph})$, as shown by the full line in Fig. 9.1. Considering the approximations involved, and the rather scanty information on some of the parameters, the agreement is surprisingly good. Note that when Landau and Khalatnikov wrote their first paper the viscosity had only been measured down to about 1·3 K.

9.2. The thermal kinetic coefficient

The thermal kinetic coefficient K is a measure of the *irreversible* flow of heat due to a temperature gradient. This flow is quite different from that due to the convection of the two fluids specified by equation (6.9). The convective flow is reversible, and does not lead to any dissipation. It is also much greater than that associated with K, hence the effects of the latter are often hard to observe. The coefficient K has the form and dimensions of a thermal conductivity, and is sometimes described as the thermal conductivity of the normal fluid, but although there is some truth in this description, it is a misleading simplification. For example if only phonons are present, K vanishes completely. Thus K depends in a very complicated way on the interactions between the excitations. The calculation of K proceeds in a similar way to that of the viscosity. The only unknown parameter is the roton interaction function and this may be deduced from the value of the roton viscosity η_r.

We cannot observe the heat transport associated with K in the presence of a steady temperature gradient as it is so much

smaller than the transport due to the relative motion of the
two fluids (section 6.7). However, its effect is obvious in the
propagation of second sound which consists of oscillations of
the two fluids in anti-phase (section 6.3). This motion is reversible, but there is a dissipation of energy associated with the
temperature gradient in the normal fluid, and this leads to

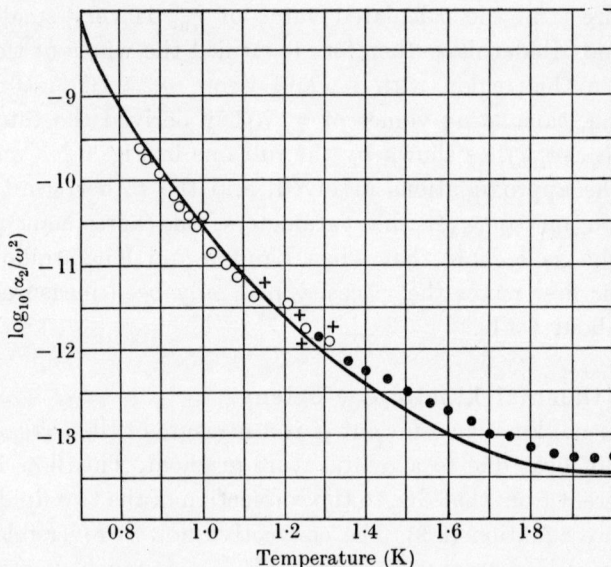

FIG. 9.2. The coefficient of absorption α_2 for second sound of angular frequency ω. ○ Zinov'eva [45]); ● Hanson and Pellam [46]; + Atkins and
Hart [47]. The full line shows calculated values. (After Khalatnikov [48].)

absorption of the second sound with a coefficient of absorption

$$\alpha = \frac{2\pi^2 f^2}{\rho c_2^3} \frac{K}{C} , \qquad (9.1)$$

where f and c_2 are the frequency and velocity of the second
sound, and ρ and C the density and specific heat of the helium.
Although other irreversible processes such as the normal
viscosity have some small effect, the absorption is associated
principally with the coefficient K; and the full line in Fig. 9.2
shows values of this absorption calculated from equation (9.1)

and the theoretical values of K. Fig. 9.2 also shows two sets of experimental values for the attenuation of waves and pulses of second sound, and we see that there is good agreement between theory and measurement. This may be somewhat fortuitous in view of the various approximations made in the calculation of the coefficient K, and because some of the necessary parameters are not known too accurately. Even so, the agreement gives substantial support to the concepts involved in the coefficient K, and to Khalatnikov's method of evaluation.

9.3. The absorption of sound

The coefficient of the absorption of ordinary sound in liquid ⁴He varies with temperature in a complex way, as shown in Fig. 9.3. We may distinguish at least three temperature regions in which the adsorption arises from quite different mechanisms. Above the lambda point, the absorption is accounted for by the usual processes of viscosity and thermal conductivity as in ordinary liquids. At the lambda point there is a very high absorption associated with the phase transition, and then a

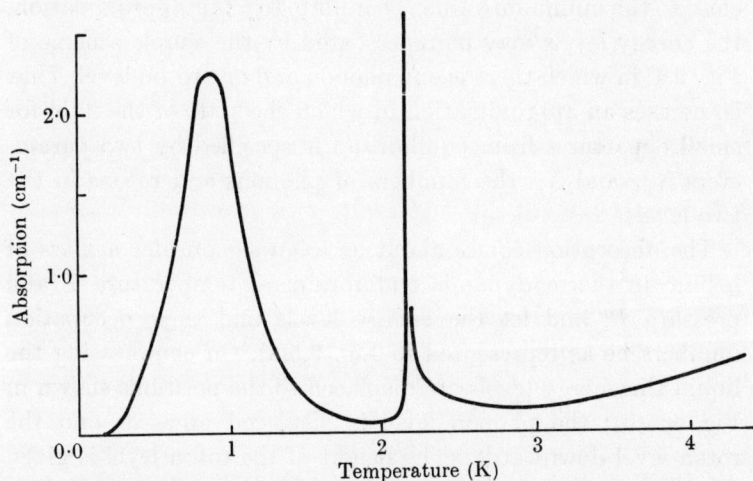

FIG. 9.3. The coefficient of absorption of 12 MHz sound waves in liquid ⁴He under the saturated vapour pressure (after Atkins [3]).

large peak in the region of 1 K. (There is also a region below
0·6 K, which we do not consider, where only phonons are
present.)

The large peak at about 1 K has been explained by Khalatnikov. In order to discuss a rather complicated situation
involving all the excitations, Khalatnikov notes that most of
the energy of the phonons is associated with the modes of
highest energy, and that most of the rotons will have an energy

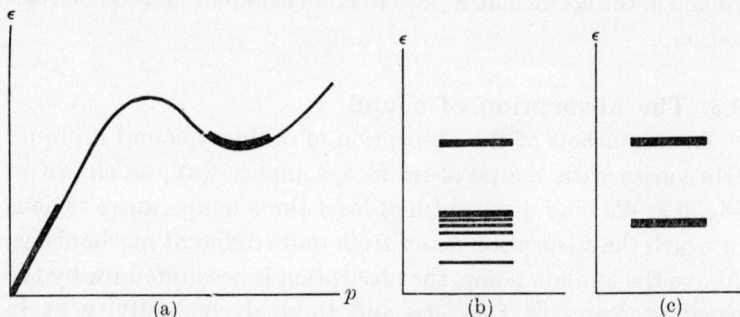

FIG. 9.4. (a) Landau's excitation spectrum for excitations in helium II.
(b) Schematic diagram of the energy levels. (c) Simplified schematic diagram
of the energy levels (after Dransfeld, Newell, and Wilks [49]).

close to the minimum value. Therefore, to a fair approximation,
the energy levels may be represented by the simple scheme of
Fig. 9.4, in which there is one phonon and one roton level. That
is, he uses an approximation in which the state of the fluid for
small departures from equilibrium is specified by two parameters N_{ph} and N_r, the numbers of phonons and rotons in the
two levels.

The absorption comes about as follows. Consider a mass of
helium in thermodynamic equilibrium at temperature T and
pressure P, and let the energy levels and their occupation
numbers be as represented in Fig. 9.5(a). On compressing the
liquid the energy levels are displaced to the positions shown in
Fig. 9.5(b); the phonon level is displaced upwards and the
roton level downwards. (The height of the roton level is given
by the parameter Δ, and $(\partial\Delta/\partial\rho)$ is known to be negative from
neutron scattering experiments.) If the compression is carried

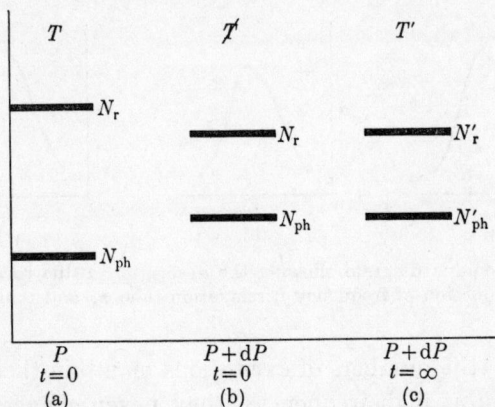

FIG. 9.5. Schematic diagram of the changes in the energy levels and occupation numbers which occur when helium II is subjected to an instantaneous pressure change (after Dransfeld, Newell, and Wilks [49]).

out rapidly, the occupation numbers N_{ph} and N_r remain unchanged, and no longer correspond to the equilibrium state for the new levels. Therefore a redistribution of energy takes place between the different modes, until the liquid is again in internal equilibrium; it will then be at a somewhat different temperature T' characterized by occupation numbers N'_{ph} and N'_r (Fig. 9.5(c)). This redistribution involves the emission and absorption of phonons and rotons, and therefore comes about via the five-phonon and phonon-roton processes of section 9.1. These processes do not happen instantaneously but are characterized by certain relaxation times. Hence, if the liquid is subjected to an alternating pressure, the numbers of excitations will lag behind their equilibrium values; the motion will be irreversible and absorption will occur. This irreversible response of a system to a change in volume is characterized by another kinetic coefficient, the so-called *second viscosity*.

The absorption at a given temperature will vary with frequency in a manner typical of all relaxation processes (Fig. 9.6(a)). That is, it has a maximum value when the period of the sound wave is comparable to the relaxation times in the liquid, and is very small at both high and low frequencies. (At low

7

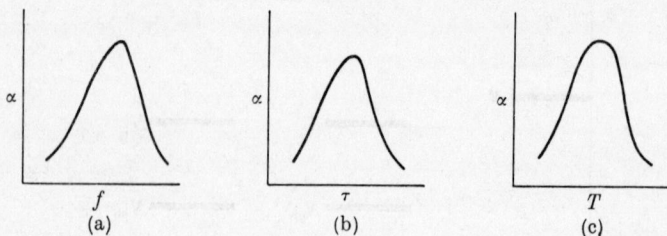

Fig. 9.6. Schematic diagram showing the absorption α due to a relaxation process as a function of frequency f, relaxation time τ, and temperature T.

frequencies, the numbers of excitations maintain their equilibrium values; at high frequencies they never change. In both cases the motion is reversible.) One might study this relaxation by working at constant frequency and somehow varying the relaxation times τ within the liquid, so tracing out a curve of the form shown schematically in Fig. 9.6(b). In fact, the relevant relaxation times change very rapidly with temperature. Hence, by working at constant frequency, and varying the temperature, we obtain the form of curve shown in Fig. 9.6(c) similar to the peak in Fig. 9.3. Khalatnikov's treatment gives a good semi-quantitative account of the observed absorption, and of its dependence on the frequency of the sound and the density of the helium. (Note, however, that a paper by Khalatnikov and Chernikova [50] suggests that the establishment of equilibrium between the phonons and rotons plays a more important part in the relaxation than is assumed in previous treatments.)

9.4. The thermal boundary resistance

In the course of Kapitza's early experiments on heat flow in helium II he attempted to measure the temperature gradient around a heated wire immersed in the bulk liquid. As the apparent conductivity of the liquid is very high, no temperature gradient could be observed in the liquid itself, but the wire ran appreciably hotter than the liquid. Kapitza also showed by an ingenious experiment that this temperature difference was located within a few hundredths of a millimetre of the surface of the wire. At the time of these experiments, the temperature drop was associated with a thermal resistance arising from the anomalous properties of helium II. However, it now appears that this so-called Kapitza resistance is merely one example of the thermal resistance which occurs at a boundary between any

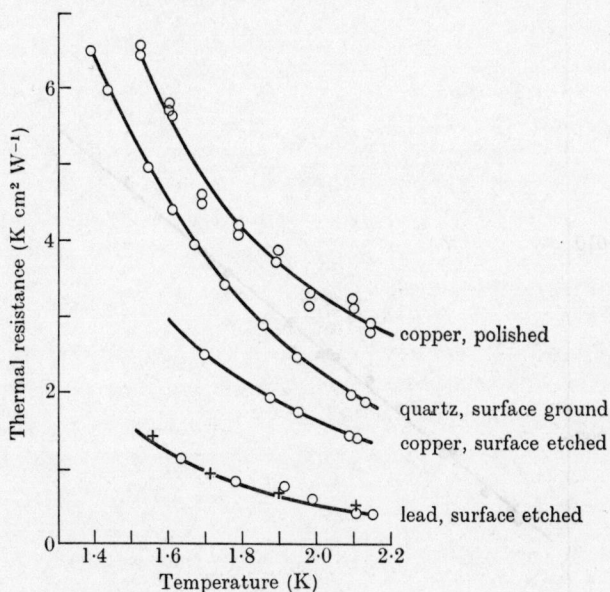

FIG. 9.7. The thermal boundary resistance between liquid helium II and copper, quartz, and lead (Challis, Dransfeld, and Wilks [51]).

two different media. The case of helium II is of particular interest because virtually all the temperature drop occurs at the boundary. In other liquids there is a considerable temperature gradient in the liquid, and it is difficult to resolve the boundary resistance from that of the bulk material.

Typical values of the boundary resistance are shown in Fig. 9.7. The heat flow depends both on the nature of the solid material and its surface finish. Hence, as it is extremely difficult to specify the nature of a surface, it is not surprising that the experimental results are not entirely reproducible. Thus the heat flow varies approximately as T^n, and for copper alone different authors report values of n varying from less than 2·5 to more than 4. We see from Fig. 9.8 that the temperature dependence of the heat flow shows no change in the region of 0·6 K, where the number of rotons begins to make a large contribution to the specific heat and normal density ρ_n. We

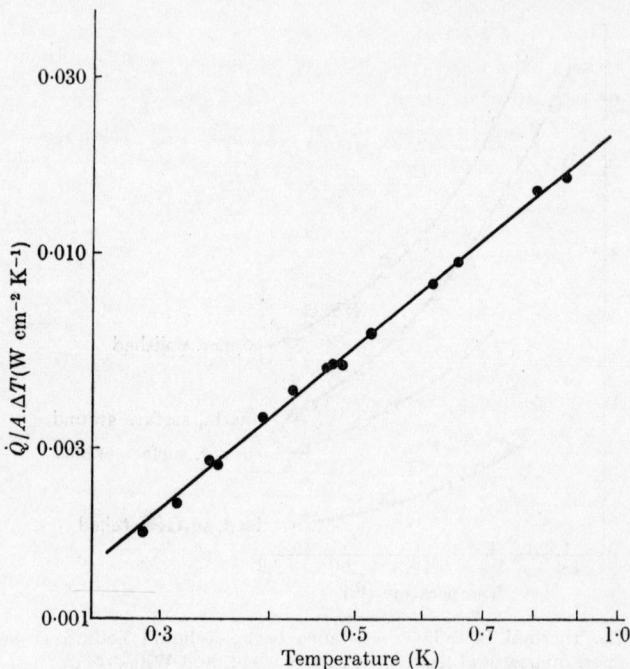

FIG. 9.8. The heat flow $\dot{Q}$ through a boundary of area A between liquid helium and copper for a temperature difference ΔT (Fairbank and Wilks [52]).

conclude that the heat flow across the boundary does not take place primarily by a mechanism characteristic of the two-fluid model. This is confirmed by measurements on the resistance between solids and liquid ^{3}He, which give results quite similar to those for ^{4}He. (Although at a temperature of about 0·01 K there is an effect with ^{3}He which is not yet understood [53].)

The nature of the mechanism of heat transfer across the boundary is still something of a mystery. It is clear that the solid surface and the helium will exchange energy by the radiation of sound waves, and a resistance will result if there is any acoustic mismatch between the two media. This approach predicts a heat flow varying with temperature as T^3, but an order of magnitude less than that observed. It seems that some additional mechanism of heat transfer must be present, but it is not clear what this is. Experimental evidence has been sought by observing the resistance as a function of the density of the helium, the effect of a superconducting transition in the solid material, and the variation of the resistance with the Debye θ of the solid. However the problem remains unsolved. For comments on the present situation see references [54] and [55].

CHAPTER X

DILUTE SOLUTIONS OF ^{3}He IN HELIUM II

ABOVE 0.8 K liquid ^{3}He and ^{4}He are miscible in all proportions, but at lower temperatures a phase separation occurs as shown in Fig. 10.1. As the temperature tends to absolute zero, the lighter

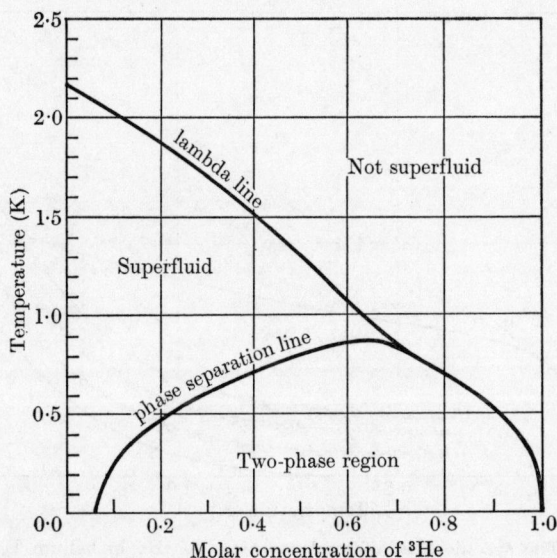

FIG. 10.1. The phase separation and lambda lines of ^{3}He-^{4}He solutions (after Taconis and De Bruyn Ouboter [56]).

phase consists of almost pure ^{3}He, while the heavier ^{4}He-rich phase contains about 6% of ^{3}He. At first sight it might seem that we have an entropy of mixing associated with this latter phase, in contradiction to the Third Law of Thermodynamics. In fact, the behaviour of the liquid mixture is governed by degenerate quantum statistics and its entropy vanishes, just as the entropy of liquid ^{3}He or liquid ^{4}He vanishes at absolute zero. In this chapter we discuss solutions sufficiently dilute that we are dealing with a liquid which is essentially helium II, but containing a little ^{3}He. We shall see that the properties of the helium II may still be described in terms of the two-fluid model, but are considerably modified by even small amounts of ^{3}He.

10.1. The specific heat

Fig. 10.2 shows the specific heat of dilute solutions of ^{3}He in helium II down to 0·3 K. We see that at low concentrations and low temperatures, the specific heat appears to be increased by an amount which, for each concentration, is independent of the

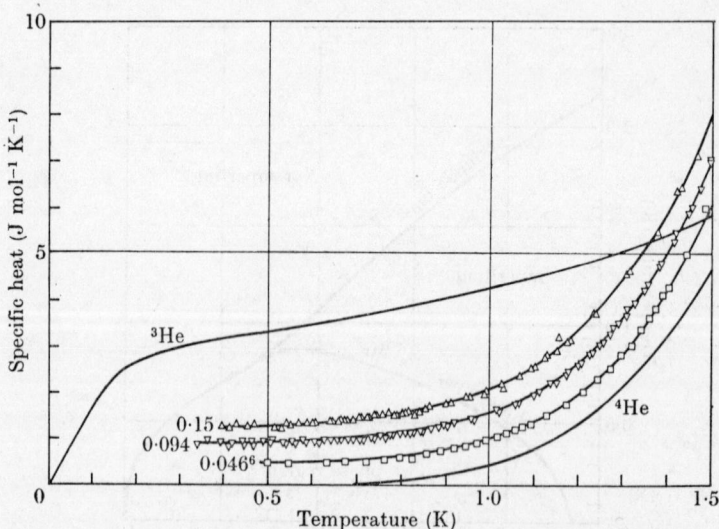

FIG. 10.2. The specific heat of weak solutions of ^{3}He in helium II at low temperatures. The figures on the three curves indicate the molar fraction of ^{3}He in the solution (De Bruyn Ouboter, Taconis, Le Pair, and Beenakker [57]).

temperature. Moreover, as the specific heat of pure helium II is very small, virtually all the specific heat of the solution is associated with the ^{3}He.

The limiting low temperature values shown in Fig. 10.2 are set out in Table 10.1, where they are compared with the value $\frac{3}{2}XR$ where X is the molar concentration of ^{3}He, and R the gas constant. We see that at low concentrations the specific heat approaches this value, suggesting that the only appreciable

TABLE 10.1

Values of the measured specific heat and $\frac{3}{2}XR$ for three different molar concentrations X (after reference [57])

X	$\frac{3}{2}XR$ (J mol^{-1} K^{-1})	$C_{\exp}$ (J mol^{-1} K^{-1})
0·15	1·871	$\approx$1·3
0·094	1·172	0·95
0·0466	0·582	0·51

thermal motion at these temperatures is a classical translational energy of $\frac{3}{2}k_BT$ per atom of ^{3}He. (At still lower temperatures, the specific heat falls well below the classical value of $\frac{3}{2}k_B$ per atom, because the ^{3}He atoms are then governed by Fermi rather than Boltzmann statistics. We mentioned this region in section 4.3, and do not consider it further in this chapter.)

10.2. ^{3}He and the normal fluid

^{3}He solute atoms do not take part in superfluid flow. We have already mentioned in section 6.6 that if helium II is allowed to run out of a vessel through a very fine capillary, only the superfluid passes through the capillary, and virtually all the normal fluid is left behind in the vessel. If we now repeat the experiment with a dilute solution in the vessel, we find that the ^{3}He atoms do not pass through the capillary, but remain behind with the normal fluid.

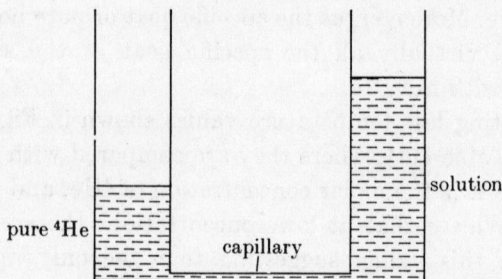

FIG. 10.3. Schematic diagram of apparatus for observing the osmotic pressure of ³He in helium II.

As ³He solute atoms do not pass through a superleak, a fine capillary may be used as a form of semi-permeable membrane to observe their osmotic pressure, as in Fig. 10.3. If both vessels are held at the same temperature to avoid any thermomechanical effects, superfluid from the left hand vessel passes through the capillary until the osmotic pressure of the ³He is balanced by the excess hydrostatic pressure. It is found that, for solutions containing up to 4 per cent of ³He, the osmotic pressure is given to within a few per cent by Van't Hoff's law

$$\Delta P_3 = \frac{n_3 R T}{V} ,$$

where n_3 is the number of moles of ³He in the volume V of the solution, and R is the gas constant. This simple relation is, of course, generally valid for all dilute solutions when the pressure is developed across a perfect semi-permeable membrane. Hence we conclude that virtually no ³He atoms pass through the capillary.

Another characteristic phenomenon associated with dilute solutions is the so-called 'heat flush' effect. If a heat current flows through a dilute solution, it is found that the ³He concentration at the cold end of the system increases, while at the hot end it decreases. Indeed, if the heat flux is sufficiently large, virtually all the ³He may be swept away from the hot end, hence the term 'heat flush'. (It is often necessary to beware of this effect when making measurements on dilute solutions!)

From the point of view of the two-fluid model, it appears that the solute atoms are dragged along by the normal fluid as it moves from the hot to the cold parts of the system.

As we have just seen, the heat flush effect suggests that the ^{3}He atoms move with the normal fluid. This is confirmed by measurements of the normal density ρ_n of dilute solutions, using Andronikashvili's method of observing the period of a pile

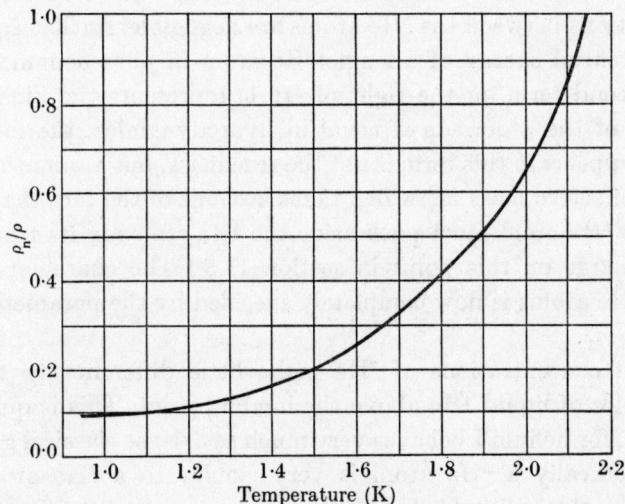

FIG. 10.4. The density of the normal fluid ρ_n in a 3·3 % (by mass) solution of ^{3}He in helium II, as a function of temperature (after Pellam [58]).

of discs oscillating in the liquid (section 6.5). In pure helium II the normal density falls off below 1 K, as the heat energy tends to zero, but in solutions the ^{3}He atoms contribute to the normal fluid, so that the normal density tends to a constant and finite value (depending on the ^{3}He concentration) as shown in Fig. 10.4. Other experiments show that this additional contribution to ρ_n is directly proportional to the concentration of ^{3}He atoms.

10.3. ^{3}He solute atoms as excitations

The experiments described in the previous section suggest that ^{3}He solute atoms behave rather as another form of excitation. They exert an osmotic pressure and cannot pass through superleaks. They contribute to the normal fluid, and are dragged along by a heat current. Like phonons and rotons, they will have an energy ϵ and a momentum p. The natural relation between these two quantities is the form originally proposed by Pomeranchuk, namely

$$\epsilon = \epsilon_{30} + p^2/2m_3^* . \qquad (10.1)$$

The solutions are assumed to be sufficiently dilute that any interactions between the ^{3}He atoms are negligible, so that ϵ_{30} is the potential energy of a single ^{3}He atom in pure helium II. The second term on the right of (10.1) represents the kinetic energy of the atom. As is usual in hydrodynamics, the mass which appears in this term is not the true mass, but a somewhat larger effective mass m_3^* which takes account of the fact that a moving ^{3}He atom must push aside the ^{4}He atoms in its track. (We enlarge on this point in section 11.5.) The character of these ^{3}He atoms is now completely specified by the parameters ϵ_{30} and m_3^*.

Small concentrations of ^{3}He make little difference to the properties of liquid ^{4}He above the lambda point. This is quite natural, for helium I behaves very much as a dense classical gas, and classically a ^{3}He atom is very similar to a ^{4}He atom. However, the position below the lambda point is quite different, and the liquid must be described in terms of elementary excitations. To anticipate the next chapter, the behaviour of helium II is the consequence of the Bose statistics and the symmetry of the wave function. All the ^{4}He atoms are indistinguishable from each other, and it is meaningless to talk of individual atoms. However, a ^{3}He solute atom is obviously distinguishable from a ^{4}He atom, and we therefore expect it to behave differently.

The essential characteristic of the ^{3}He solute atoms is that they are *different* from the ^{4}He atoms; the fact that they obey Fermi-Dirac rather than Bose statistics is irrelevant. This point is not too easy to demonstrate experimentally as the only substance soluble in helium II and obeying Bose statistics is the isotope ^{6}He, which has a half-life of only 0·8 second!

Even so, it appears that this isotope does not take part in superfluid flow (Guttman and Arnold [59]).

10.4. Some dynamic properties

We now briefly indicate some of the principal ways in which ^{3}He solute atoms modify the dynamic behaviour of helium II. Fig. 10.5 shows the effect of 1% of ^{3}He on the normal viscosity η_n. The observed decrease comes about because the viscosity is proportional to the mean free path of the excitations, which is reduced by the ^{3}He atoms scattering the excitations. The effect is most marked at lower temperatures where the excitations are less numerous and produce less scattering themselves, so that the role of the ^{3}He is relatively more important.

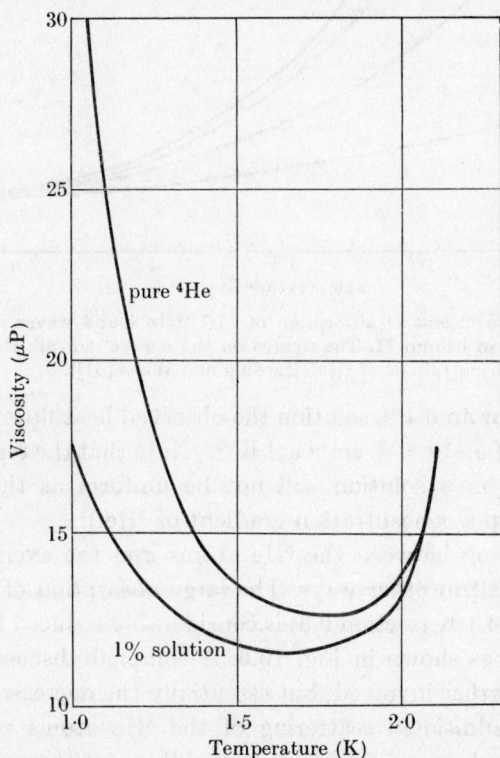

FIG. 10.5. The effect of 1% molar concentration of ^{3}He on the normal viscosity η_n of helium II (Staas, Taconis, and Fokkens [60]).

The effect of ^{3}He atoms on the heat flow is even more marked. The moving normal fluid sweeps the ^{3}He atoms to the cold part of the system, where they build up a concentration gradient tending to diffuse back to the warmer region. Scattering between these atoms and the normal fluid acts as a resistance to the flow of the normal fluid, which greatly reduces the heat

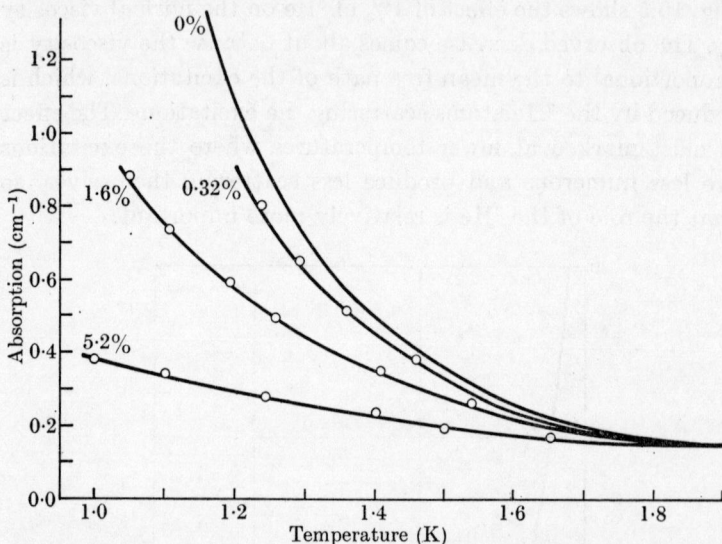

FIG. 10.6. The coefficient of absorption of 14·7 MHz sound waves in dilute solutions of ^{3}He in helium II. The figures on the curves indicate the molar concentrations of ^{3}He (Harding and Wilks [61]).

flux. In fact for an 0·1% solution the observed heat flow is only of the order of 5×10^{-3} W cm^{-1} s^{-1} K^{-1}. (Note that the temperature gradient in a solution will not be uniform as the heat current sets up a concentration gradient of ^{3}He.)

The scattering between the ^{3}He atoms and the excitations also shows itself in other ways. The large absorption of sound in the region of 1 K (section 9.3) is considerably reduced by ^{3}He solute atoms, as shown in Fig. 10.6. A complete discussion of this effect is rather involved, but essentially the decrease arises because the additional scattering of the ^{3}He atoms permits equilibrium to be established more rapidly, and thus reduces the irreversibility associated with the changes of pressure.

We have already noted (section 8.5) that the propagation of second sound becomes impossible at some temperature below 1 K when the mean free path of the excitations becomes comparable with the wavelength of the sound. An addition of ³He solute atoms reduces the mean free path, and therefore permits the observation of second sound to lower temperatures. Fig. 10.7 shows the received signal when a 20 μs heat pulse is transmitted through pure helium II at 0·45 K, and through a 0·32% solution at the same temperature. In the first case the

(a)

(b)

FIG. 10.7. The shape of heat pulses transmitted through liquid helium and viewed on an oscilloscope trace: (a) pure ⁴He at 0·45 K, (b) ⁴He containing 0·32% ³He at 0·45 K (after King and Fairbank [62]).

shape of the pulse is characteristic of ordinary (Fourier) heat propagation, whereas the quite sharp pulse in the solution is characteristic of second sound. The velocity of second sound is also modified by ³He solute atoms. This comes about partly because the normal density is greatly increased at the lower temperatures (Fig. 10.4), and also because the equations of motion of the liquid (section 6.2) must be extended to include two additional equations to specify the conservation of the ³He atoms, and their effect on the chemical potential of the liquid.

10.5. Ions in helium II

We now refer briefly to some experiments involving the motion of positive and negative helium ions in liquid helium II, which can be produced in small concentrations by the action of suitable ionizing radiation. Their motion may then be directed by electric fields, and detected by measuring the resulting current, as first shown by Carreri, Scaramuzzi, and Thomson. As both the positive and negative ions are different from the uncharged ⁴He atoms, we expect them to behave in rather the same way as ^{3}He solute atoms. In principle, a study of these ions should yield more information than experiments on ^{3}He solutions, because their motion is more easily observed. However, the theoretical treatment is more complicated because the ions appear to be complexes of helium atoms held together by electric polarization charges.

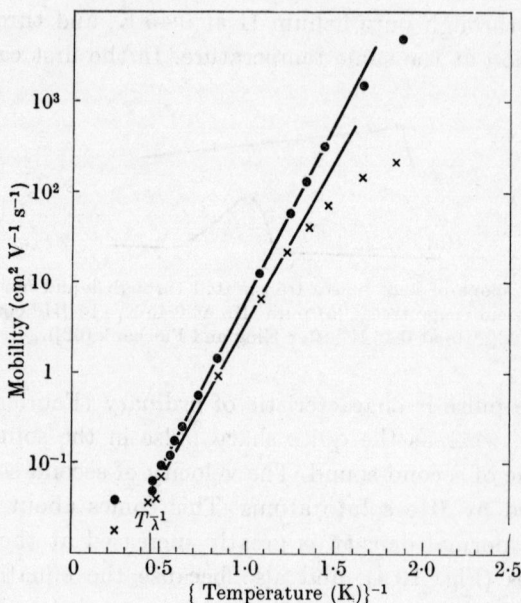

F I G. 10.8. The mobility of ions in liquid ^{4}He: ●, positive ions; ×, negative ions (Reif and Meyer [63]).

The most important parameter characterizing an ion in solution is its mobility, which is defined as

$$\mu = v_d/E,$$

where v_d is the drift velocity in an applied field E. This mobility is measured by observing the time of flight of ions between two electrodes, and values for ions in helium II are shown in Fig. 10.8. The temperature dependence is much greater than that exhibited by the mobilities of ions in liquid helium I and liquid ^{3}He. The straight lines in Fig. 10.8 correspond to expressions of the form $\mu = \alpha \exp(\Delta/k_B T)$ where $\Delta/k_B = 8\cdot 8$ K and $8\cdot 1$ K for positive and negative ions respectively. It appears that the ions are scattered primarily by the rotons, so that their mean free path is inversely proportional to the number of rotons, which varies approximately as $\exp(-\Delta/k_B T)$. Below about $0\cdot 7$ K the mobility increases less rapidly with falling temperature, probably because of residual scattering by phonons and the other ions.

The nature of the ions is rather complex. Thus, the mobilities in Fig. 10.8 show that the positive and negative ions have a different form. At the low concentrations involved, we expect the ions to obey Boltzmann statistics, so the diffusion constant should be related to the mobility by the classical Nernst-Einstein relation

$$D = (k_B T/e)\mu,$$

where e is the electronic charge. This relation predicts a value of D of about 3×10^{-5} c.g.s. at $1\cdot 4$ K, which contrasts with the corresponding value for ^{3}He atoms of about 10^{-3} c.g.s. This low value suggests that the ions consist of large groups of atoms held together by polarization charges, as mentioned above. The difference in behaviour of the positive and negative ions presents an interesting problem not yet resolved.

One application of the above technique has been to study the motion of a small concentration of ions in a heat current flowing in helium II. The ions were acted on by electric fields transverse to the direction of the heat flow. The magnitude and direction of the ionic velocities were then deduced by observing the deflection of the ion currents flowing to a number of separate collector electrodes. Hence, using the values of the mobility given above, it could be demonstrated that in the absence of a field, the ions move with the velocity of the normal fluid, as we have already assumed for ^{3}He solute atoms. We refer to other experiments using ions in Chapters 12 and 14.

10.6. The dilution refrigerator

The usual method of maintaining a low temperature is by the evaporation of low boiling point liquids. Thus a temperature bath between 4 and 1 K is readily obtained by pumping on liquid ^{4}He in a dewar vessel. To maintain the same cooling capacity at a lower temperature, we must evaporate the same amount of liquid at a lower pressure by using a larger pumping system. However, the saturated vapour pressure decreases very rapidly with temperature, so we soon reach a practical limit to the size of the pumping system, and to the lowest temperature obtainable. In the case of liquid ^{4}He this is about 1 K, but ^{3}He has a higher vapour pressure on account of the zero-point energy, so temperatures down to about 0·3 K are quite possible. As ^{3}He is only obtainable in relatively small quantities, it is usual to operate a ^{3}He bath within a larger cryostat maintained at about 1 K by a much larger quantity of ^{4}He. Details of such ^{3}He cryostats are given in reference [64].

Hitherto measurements below 0·3 K have been obtained only by the somewhat involved method of magnetic cooling, but the dilution refrigerator first proposed by H. London now offers the possibility of obtaining steady temperatures down to a few millikelvins. The essence of the method is to dilute a ^{3}He–^{4}He mixture, which has separated into two phases, with pure ^{4}He. This dilution is accompanied by a negative heat of mixing, and hence by considerable cooling. How does this cooling come about? The pure ^{4}He added to the mixture cannot dissolve in the ^{3}He–rich phase as this is already saturated with ^{4}He. The additional ^{4}He therefore goes to increase the volume of the ^{4}He–rich phase, while at the same time ^{3}He atoms from the ^{3}He–rich phase pass into the ^{4}He–rich phase, so as to maintain the equilibrium concentration. As we have already explained, solute atoms of ^{3}He in helium II behave rather as the molecules of a perfect gas. Hence we can imagine that, during the dilution, ^{3}He atoms 'evaporate' from the ^{3}He–rich phase into the ^{4}He–rich phase. Hence, the observed heat of mixing is analogous to the heat of evaporation of an ordinary liquid.

In practice, considerable ingenuity has to be shown to devise a refrigeration cycle which will operate continuously and with some approach to the theoretical efficiency. A good introductory account of the principles of the refrigerator is given in reference

[65], and details of construction and operation in references [66] and [67]. Note that in practice the cooling cycles operate by circulating the ^{3}He rather than the ^{4}He, (as is rather suggested by our outline of the principles involved). Steady temperatures down to 0·04 K are now fairly readily available, while a non-continuous system has reached a temperature of 4 millikelvins (Vilches and Wheatley [68]).

CHAPTER XI

WAVE FUNCTIONS OF HELIUM II

WE have already related many of the properties of helium II to the form of the excitation spectrum. We now outline Feynman's demonstration of why the excitation spectrum takes its characteristic form (Feynman [69, 70]).

11.1. The ground state of helium II and phonons

The liquid has a very open structure, in which the atoms may pass easily from one configuration to another. Even in the ground state at absolute zero, the atoms are not at rest, for they have considerable kinetic energy arising from the zero-point motion (section 1.1). The strong repulsive forces ensure that atoms do not overlap, while the attractive forces have much less influence. In fact, we may think of the atoms as a collection of hard spheres, able to move about freely, and with a tendency to take up a fairly uniform distribution.

The wave function φ of the ground state will be a definite though complicated function of the coordinates R_i of the N atoms. The value of $|\varphi(R_1, R_2, \ldots, R_N)|^2$ indicates the probability of finding the atoms in the ground state in the particular configuration $R_1, R_2, \ldots, R_N$. As described above, the atoms are free to move about in the liquid subject only to the condition that they must not overlap. Hence the value of φ must tend to zero for configurations in which atoms approach too closely. Moreover, just as the wave function for a particle in a box has its maximum value when the particle is at the centre of the box, and furthest from the walls, we expect the maximum value of φ to be for configurations in which the atoms keep well apart. In simple systems for which the Schrödinger equation has been solved completely, it turns out that the eigenfunctions have real values. We therefore assume that φ is real. In addition, ground-state wave functions have no nodes, hence we assume φ to have a positive value for all configurations of the atoms.

Feynman now discusses the wave functions of the excited states in a manner which gives nearly all the information we require about them, without having to calculate the complicated ground-state function. He begins by considering the low energy excitations which we know to be phonons. The equations of motion of sound vibrations expressed in normal coordinates are analogous to those of the harmonic oscillator. The wave function of the ground state of a linear harmonic oscillator with position coordinate x is a Gaussian function $\exp(-\tfrac{1}{2}\alpha x^2)$. The coordinate x fluctuates on account of zero-point motion, and the probability of a fluctuation of given amplitude falls off as the exponential of the square of the amplitude. The wave function of the first excited state is $x \exp(-\tfrac{1}{2}\alpha x^2)$, which is just the ground-state function multiplied by the position coordinate. Feynman recalls that the classical normal coordinate appropriate to sound waves in a liquid may be written

$$\rho_k = \int \rho(\mathbf{R})\exp(ik \cdot \mathbf{R})\, d^3\mathbf{R},$$

where $\rho(\mathbf{R})$ is the number density, or alternatively, if we replace $\rho(\mathbf{R})$ by a quantum mechanical density operator,

$$\rho_k = \sum_i \exp(ik \cdot \mathbf{R}_i).$$

(The first term in the bracket has the usual value $\sqrt{-1}$, and should not be confused with the subscripts associated with the summation.) By analogy with the harmonic oscillator, Feynman now writes the excited state wave function as the ground-state function φ multiplied by ρ_k, that is

$$\psi_{\text{ph}} = \left\{\sum_i \exp(i\mathbf{k} \cdot \mathbf{R}_i)\right\}\varphi. \qquad (11.1)$$

It is not immediately obvious that the wave function (11.1) represents a density variation. However, we recall that the ground-state function corresponds to a great range of possibilities for the configurations of the atoms, some being more probable than others. Consider the real part of (11.1),

$$\left\{\sum_i \cos(i\mathbf{k} \cdot \mathbf{R}_i)\right\}\varphi.$$

It might seem that the cosine term will be positive for exactly half the number of configurations (sets of values $\mathbf{R}_1$, $\mathbf{R}_2$, ..., $\mathbf{R}_N$), and negative for the other half. In this case the function would vanish. However, the zero-point motion of the ground state can be regarded as an assembly of density fluctuations. The term $\sum_i \cos(i\mathbf{k} \cdot \mathbf{R}_i)$ therefore picks out from the ground state just those fluctuations corresponding to phonons of wave number $\mathbf{k}$.

11.2. The scarcity of excited states

We now consider what other forms of excitations besides phonons are permitted in the liquid. As any density fluctuations may be described in terms of phonons, any other excitations must involve motions of the atoms at approximately constant density. As already noted, a wide range of configurations is available to the atoms, because of the very open structure of the liquid. Feynman therefore assumes the atoms can readily be moved from one configuration to another by some type of stirring process. To transfer the system from the ground state to an excited state involves rearranging the atoms into some new configuration. Our problem is to deduce the wave function of this configuration.

According to the general properties of the Schrödinger equation, the wave function of a stationary excited state ψ is orthogonal to the ground-state function φ. As φ is everywhere positive, ψ must be positive for some configurations $(\mathbf{R_1}, \mathbf{R_2}, \ldots, \mathbf{R}_N)$ and negative for others. Thus, if ψ is plotted against the $3N$ coordinates of configuration space, it will vary between certain maximum positive and negative values. We are concerned in the first place with states of low energy, and the criterion for such states is that the gradient of ψ in configuration space should be small. (The wave function of a particle in a box oscillates more frequently the higher the energy, as the kinetic energy is given by $-(\hbar^2/2m)\nabla^2\psi$.)

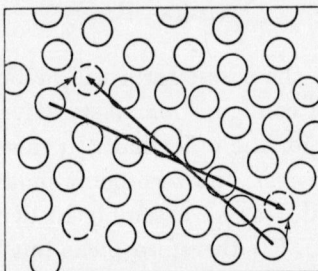

Fig. 11.1. The effect of two large displacements of the atoms (long arrows), can actually be accomplished by much smaller adjustments (short arrows) because of the identity of the atoms (Feynman [70]).

Let us refer to the configuration which gives ψ its maximum positive value as an A configuration, and that which gives the maximum negative value as a B configuration. Then if ψ is to represent a state of low energy, the points corresponding to configurations A and B should be widely separated in configuration space. If the atoms are distinguishable, this condition implies that to move atoms from an A configuration to a B configuration involves a stirring process in which all the atoms are displaced a long way. However, as all the atoms of the liquid are indistinguishable and obey Bose statistics, the wave function must remain unchanged by any permutation of the atoms. Hence it is possible to go from an A configuration to a B, or indeed to any other one, by moving each atom by a distance of no more than about the atomic spacing (see Fig. 11.1). This means that configurations A and B can only be separated by a certain limited distance in configuration space, the energy cannot be made arbitrarily small, and will not drop below a certain minimum value.

The above argument shows that some minimum energy is required to create excitations other than phonons. In particular we have ruled out the possibility of particle-like excitations with a spectrum $\epsilon = p^2/2m$. It also follows that the number of non-phonon excitations present in the liquid will decrease exponentially as the temperature is reduced. Hence at sufficiently low temperatures only phonons will be present. Note that the above conclusions will not apply to liquid ^{3}He, which obeys Fermi-Dirac statistics. The wave function then changes sign if we permute atoms, and it is very difficult to see what happens using this approach. The behaviour of ^{4}He is a consequence of the symmetry of the wave functions of a Bose system.

11.3. Feynman's variational method

In this section we describe Feynman's method for deducing the form of the excitation spectrum. This is based on the variational method. If a system has a Hamiltonian H, and ψ is any wave function orthogonal to the ground state, then the energy of the first excited state

$$E' \leqslant \frac{\int \psi^* H \psi \, d\tau}{\int \psi^* \psi \, d\tau} . \tag{11.2}$$

The equality sign is valid only if ψ is an exact eigenfunction of H. As a completely general expression equation (11.2) is not particularly useful. Suppose, however, that we have a system for which the Schrödinger equation is very complicated, but for which we think we can guess an approximate wave function ψ. Then, if we guess well, the upper limit for E' given by (11.2) may be quite close to the true value. We may go further by expressing our trial wave function ψ in terms of some parameter or parameters which are of physical significance for the problem in question. In this case, if we vary the parameters so as to minimize the right-hand side of (11.2), we may expect the function ψ to become a better approximation to the true solution.

Feynman begins by choosing a trial wave function to describe an excitation in the liquid. Fig. 11.2 shows schematically the sites of the atoms (labelled α and β) corresponding to the A and B configurations which give ψ its maximum positive and negative values (cf. section 11.2). In order to obtain the states of lowest energy, an α-site must be as far away as possible from a

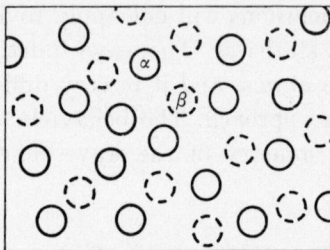

FIG. 11.2. The excited state wave function is positive for the configuration shown by solid circles (α-sites), and negative for the dotted circles (β-sites). For the lowest energy, all the β-sites must be as far as possible from the α-sites (Feynman [70]).

β-site. Yet because of the Bose statistics, no α-site can be more than an atomic spacing from the corresponding β-site, hence the A and B configurations are quite similar. They will be farthest from each other in configuration space if it is necessary to move every atom to effect a transition between the two. That is, if all the α-sites are between β-sites, as shown in the figure.

The states of the system with lowest energy will be those in which the wave function varies smoothly as the atoms pass from an A to B configuration. To ensure this, the amplitude of ψ is taken to be the number of atoms on α-sites minus the number of atoms on β-sites. This number is $\sum_i f(\mathbf{R}_i)$ where $f(\mathbf{R})$ is a function which is $+1$ if $\mathbf{R}$ defines an α-site, and -1 if $\mathbf{R}$ defines a β-site, and which varies smoothly between these limits. We have also the condition that the atoms must not overlap, so, bearing in mind our treatment of the phonons, we choose as the trial function

$$\psi = \left\{ \sum_i f(\mathbf{R}_i) \right\} \varphi, \tag{11.3}$$

where φ is again the ground-state function, which takes account of correlations between the atoms. Although Feynman does not specify the motion of the atoms more precisely than by this last equation, he points out that (11.3) is consistent with three quite probable modes of motion, viz. the rotation of a small ring of atoms, the excitation of single atoms in a cage, and single atoms vibrating while the surrounding atoms move about to get out of their path.

The variational method is now used to determine the best form of the function $\sum_i f(\mathbf{R}_i)$. The Hamiltonian of the liquid is taken to be

$$H = -(\hbar^2/2m) \sum_i \nabla_i^2 + V - E_\varphi,$$

where V is the potential energy of the system, and E_φ the energy of the ground state. After a rather long calculation, the ground state φ drops out, and we find that

$$f(\mathbf{R}) = \exp i(\mathbf{k} \cdot \mathbf{R}), \tag{11.4}$$

which leads to an energy

$$E(k) = \hbar^2 k^2 / 2m S(k) \tag{11.5}$$

where $S(k)$ is the Fourier transform of the two-atom correlation function $p(\mathbf{R})$. This latter function is related to the probability of finding an atom at a certain distance from a given atom, and may be determined from X-ray scattering measurements. The form of $S(k)$ is shown in Fig. 11.3.

11.4. Feynman's first wave function

Substituting values of $S(k)$ into the expression for the excitation spectrum (11.5), we obtain curve A of Fig. 11.4. The curve reproduces qualitatively the main feature of the results from the neutron scattering experiments, but the heights of the maximum and minimum are much too high.

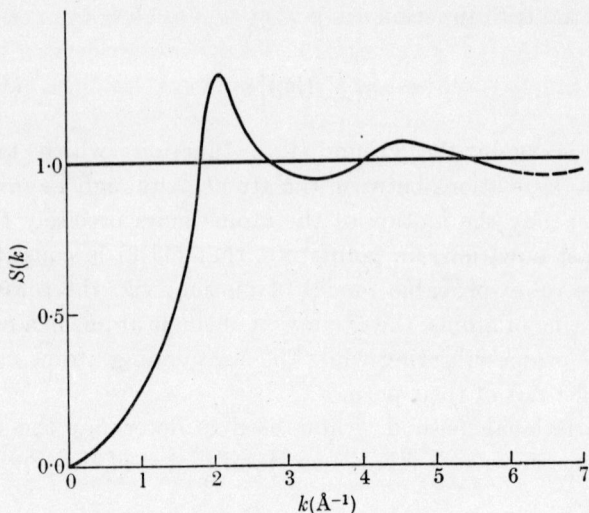

FIG. 11.3. The liquid structure factor $S(k)$ (Feynman and Cohen [71]).

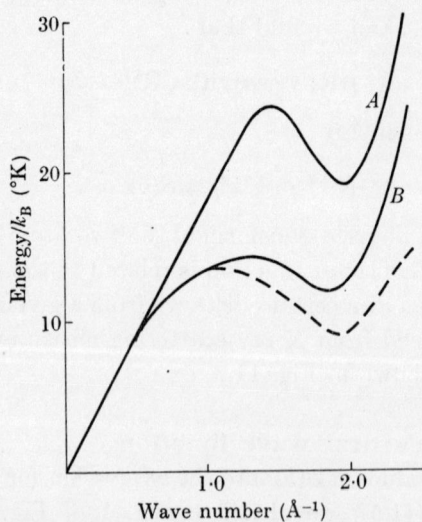

FIG. 11.4. The energy spectrum of excitations in helium II. Curve A as calculated by Feynman [69]; curve B as calculated by Feynman and Cohen; dashed line as determined by neutron scattering experiments. (After Feynman and Cohen [71].)

The variational method satisfactorily reproduces the phonon spectrum for the lower values of k. Yet it is disconcerting that the wave function obtained by substituting (11.4) into (11.3), namely

$$\psi = \left\{ \sum_i \exp(\mathbf{ik} \cdot \mathbf{R}_i) \right\} \varphi, \tag{11.6}$$

is for *all* values of $\mathbf{k}$ identical with the function we deduced for phonons in section 11.1. Clearly the excitations of higher wave number are not phonons, because the dispersion relation is quite different. This discrepancy, like that in Fig. 11.4, shows that the wave function (11.6) is not a good approximation at high values of $\mathbf{k}$.

We note that the excitations specified by (11.6) are not localized, but have the form of plane waves passing through the liquid. However, they may be localized, just as the phonons in section 7.1, by making up wave packets with linear combinations of wave functions.

11.5. ³He solutions and the two-fluid model

At this stage it is instructive to refer to some of Feynman's calculations on the behaviour of a ³He atom dissolved in helium II at absolute zero. As we saw in Chapter 10, a ³He solute atom behaves in many ways as a particular form of excitation. However, for reasons which become apparent as we proceed, it is much easier to form a physical picture of the motion of a ³He atom than of an excitation like a roton.

As the ³He atom is distinguishable from all the ⁴He atoms, it is not subject to the Bose statistics, there are few restrictions on its motion, and it has an energy spectrum of the normal classical form

$$\epsilon = p^2/2m_3^*. \tag{11.7}$$

However, the mass m_3^* is not the actual, but the effective, mass of the atom. As the ³He atom passes through the helium II it displaces ⁴He atoms which must move out of its way to let it pass. Therefore an acceleration of the ³He atom involves the acceleration of nearby ⁴He atoms. Hence, the apparent mass of the ³He atom will be greater than its actual mass, as was shown by the experiments described in Chapter 10. This effect follows from classical hydrodynamics. A sphere moving through a perfect irrotational fluid experiences no frictional force whatever, but its apparent mass is augmented by a certain factor (which for a sphere in a liquid of the same density has the value 1·5).

Consider now a collection of small spheres (or ³He atoms) moving in an irrotational fluid (or helium II at absolute zero). The ³He atoms will collide with each other and with the walls of the container, and in accord with (11.7) will exchange energy and momentum as would free particles. There is no frictional force with the helium II, hence the ³He atoms will appear to behave as a gas of particles of energy $\epsilon = p^2/2m_3^*$ moving freely in a vacuum. Thus the atoms form the 'normal fluid' associated with a solution at absolute zero. In addition there are other motions in the liquid which carry energy and momentum, namely the motions of the helium II as it flows out of the way of the ³He atoms. This flow is irrotational and does not give rise to any viscous effects. Thus the total motion of the solution falls naturally into the two divisions of the two-fluid model.

The wave function for a ³He atom moving freely through the liquid without any backflow would be

$$\psi = \{\exp(\mathbf{i}\mathbf{k} \cdot \mathbf{R}_{\mathrm{A}})\}\varphi,$$

where $\mathbf{R}_{\mathrm{A}}$ is the coordinate of the atom. We may readily verify that this function leads to an energy $\hbar^2 k^2/2m_3$, where m_3 is the actual mass of the atom. To take account of the backflow Feynman assumes another term in the wave function so that

$$\psi = \{\exp(\mathbf{i}\mathbf{k} \cdot \mathbf{R}_{\mathrm{A}})\}\Big\{\exp \mathrm{i} \sum_{i \neq \mathrm{A}} s(\mathbf{R}_i - \mathbf{R}_{\mathrm{A}})\Big\}\varphi, \qquad (11.8)$$

this expression being chosen so that the motion is irrotational and has a physically realistic form (cf. section 11.7).

Substituting (11.8) into the variational principle, we find that the requirement of minimum energy leads to a differential equation for $s(\mathbf{R})$ which for large values of $\mathbf{R}$ has the solution

$$s(\mathbf{R}) = A\mathbf{k} \cdot \mathbf{R}/R^3, \qquad (11.9)$$

where A is some constant. We may now hope to obtain the lowest value of the energy by substituting for $s(\mathbf{R})$ in (11.8) and determining the value of A by carrying out another variation. After some heavy calculations it is found that

$$E = 0.648\hbar^2 k^2/2m_3,$$

which corresponds to an effective mass of $1.55m_3$. This value for the energy is still too high, the effective mass determined experimentally being about $2.5m_3$. This discrepancy is not altogether surprising because, quite apart from the correctness of the wave function, several approximations are involved in the calculations. Thus we require the correlation functions for the ^{4}He atoms around the ^{3}He atom but this information is not available. Feynman and Cohen therefore assume that these functions are the same as for ^{4}He atoms around another ^{4}He atom, but this is obviously not exact.

11.6. Feynman and Cohen's wave function

The description of a ^{3}He solute atom in the previous section suggests a possible form of wave function for a roton. Let us picture a ^{3}He atom moving through helium II with an energy of about 9 K, the motion being accompanied by an irrotational backflow. If we now replace the ^{3}He atom by a ^{4}He atom we obtain some sort of excitation probably not very different from a roton. However, as we can no longer distinguish between any of the atoms, we must use a purely quantum mechanical description.

Any system of Bose particles must be described by a symmetrical wave function. Therefore Feynman and Cohen [71] suggest that the wave function for the situation described in the previous paragraph is obtained by symmetrizing (11.8) and writing

$$\psi = \left\{ \sum_i \exp(i\mathbf{k} \cdot \mathbf{R}_i) \right\}\left\{ \exp i \sum_{j \neq i} s(\mathbf{R}_i - \mathbf{R}_j) \right\}\varphi. \qquad (11.10)$$

The energy spectrum is obtained by inserting (11.9) and (11.10) into the variational equations, and finding the best value for A. After some computation the second excitation curve shown in Fig. 11.4 is obtained. It is clearly a big improvement over the earlier spectrum (11.5), but still gives too high an energy at the roton minimum. (Thus the calculated value of Δ/k_B is 11·5 K compared with the value of 8·65 K from the neutron scattering experiments.) However, taking into account the complexity of the calculations, the agreement must be regarded as fairly satisfactory.

Phonons are associated with the vibrational motions of the atoms, but no such simple picture seems possible for the rotons. We may visualize a ^{3}He solute atom moving through helium II, but this simple physical picture vanishes when we symmetrize the wave function to describe pure ^{4}He. However, the discussion of the last two sections suggests that a roton is essentially one ^{4}He atom travelling rapidly through the other atoms which move out of its path.

11.7. Superfluid flow

We have now completed our discussion of the thermal motions of the atoms. However, to obtain a complete description of the liquid, we also require wave functions to describe motion on a macroscopic scale, that is, to describe the liquid when we say that it is flowing. We begin by considering the behaviour of the liquid at absolute zero. As a simple example of such motion, the entire fluid may move as a body with velocity $\mathbf{v}_s$. In this case, the centre of gravity coordinates may be separated out, and the wave function written

$$\psi = \{\exp \mathrm{i}(m/\hbar)\mathbf{v}_s \cdot \sum_i \mathbf{R}_i\}\varphi, \qquad (11.11)$$

where, as before, φ corresponds to the ground state at rest in the laboratory system of coordinates.

We now represent more complex flow situations in the liquid, where the velocity $\mathbf{v}_s(\mathbf{R})$ varies from point to point, but only very gradually on an atomic scale. If we consider the atoms in a small region about a point P, the motion of their centre of gravity may be allocated a velocity $\mathbf{v}_P$. These atoms will make a contribution to the phase term of (11.11) equal to

$$(m/\hbar)\mathbf{v}_P \cdot \sum_i \mathbf{R}_i,$$

the summation being taken over all the atoms in the region. Other regions will give corresponding contributions, so the total phase factor will be $(m/\hbar) \sum \mathbf{v}(\mathbf{R}_i) \cdot \mathbf{R}_i$, the summation now being taken over all the atoms of the liquid. Thus the wave function of the whole liquid will be of the form

$$\psi = \left\{ \exp i \sum_i s(\mathbf{R}_i) \right\} \varphi, \qquad (11.12)$$

where $s(\mathbf{R}_i)$ is some function of position. The above argument suggests that $s(\mathbf{R})$ is equal to $(m/\hbar)\mathbf{v}(\mathbf{R}) \cdot \mathbf{R}$, the local velocity then being equal to the phase factor in (11.12) divided by $(m/\hbar)\mathbf{R}$. However, the wavelength of a wave will in general vary from point to point, so the velocity should be found by taking the gradient of the phase, viz.

$$\mathbf{v}_s(\mathbf{R}) = (\hbar/m)\nabla s(\mathbf{R}). \qquad (11.13)$$

We shall use this result in section 12.5.

CHAPTER XII

ROTATION AND VORTEX LINES

IN setting up the two-fluid model in Chapter 6 we included the condition

$$\operatorname{curl} \mathbf{v}_s = 0,$$

which ensures that the superfluid exhibits no turbulence. However, this relation imposes other severe restrictions on the possible modes of motion.

12.1. The rotation of simply connected systems

Let us consider a mass of helium in a simple cylindrical vessel or bucket which is rotating about its axis with a uniform angular velocity ω. To simplify matters we begin with temperatures sufficiently low that $\rho_s \simeq \rho$, so that to a good approximation $\mathbf{v}_s \simeq \mathbf{v}$, the velocity of the helium itself. The condition curl $\mathbf{v}_s = 0$ then implies that the helium must everywhere be at rest.

To see how the above result comes about, we introduce the *circulation*, which is defined as the integral

$$\oint \mathbf{v} \cdot d\mathbf{l} \tag{12.1}$$

taken over any closed circuit in a fluid. According to Stoke's law, the circulation round any *infinitesimal* circuit in a liquid may be written

$$\oint \mathbf{v} \cdot d\mathbf{l} = \oint \text{curl } \mathbf{v} \cdot d\mathbf{S}. \tag{12.2}$$

If we now expand the infinitesimal circuit via any path through the liquid, the form of (12.2) is such that it remains valid for the larger circuits so created. Alternatively we can say that (12.2) is valid for any *reducible* circuit in the liquid, that is for a circuit which can be shrunk to a point.

All possible circuits in a *simply connected region* as in a bucket, are reducible. (The liquid in the annular space between two concentric cylinders is *multiply connected*, and a circuit embracing the inner cylinder is not reducible.) Hence for helium in a simple bucket, equation (12.2) and the condition curl $\mathbf{v}_s = 0$ imply that

$$\oint \mathbf{v}_s \cdot d\mathbf{l} = 0. \tag{12.3}$$

This condition of zero circulation can only be satisfied if $\mathbf{v}_s$ vanishes everywhere. This conclusion is in accord with Andronikashvili's experiment with a pile of oscillating discs (section 6.5) where it appears that the superfluid does not take part in the rotational motion, but remains at rest. However, we now describe experiments which show that the whole mass of helium II in a bucket can be set into a state of uniform rotation.

An experiment due to Osborne used the apparatus shown in Fig. 12.1. A vertical glass tube was mounted between point

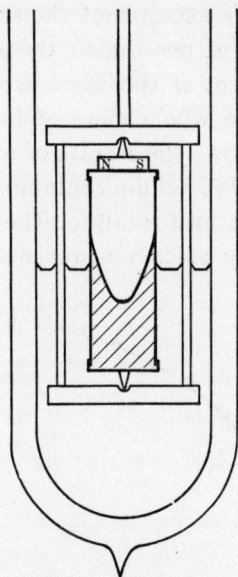

FIG. 12.1. Apparatus for observing the meniscus of rotating
helium (Osborne [72]).

bearings at top and bottom, and carried a small horizontal bar
magnet. The assembly was rotated at speeds between 8 and 16
rev s^{-1} by an external magnetic field, and the profile of the
meniscus viewed with a cathetometer through slits in the
silvering of the dewar vessels. For a normal liquid the free
surface would have a parabolic form given by

$$z = \frac{\omega^2}{2g}r^2,$$

where z and r are the vertical and radial coordinates of a point in
the surface, and ω is the angular velocity. If only a fraction
ρ_n/ρ of the helium rotates, then the centrifugal force will be
reduced in this ratio, while the gravitational forces are of
course unchanged. Hence at temperatures below 1·5 K the
height of the meniscus should be reduced by a factor of at
least ten. Osborne found that the helium II behaved as an
ordinary liquid, and we conclude that both the normal and
superfluids were rotating.

In Andronikashvili's experiment the superfluid between the pile of discs remained at rest during the oscillations. However, the position is different if the discs are steadily rotated for some seconds, for the whole mass of liquid is then set into rotation. Fig. 12.2 shows the results of an experiment, due to Hall, in which a vessel of helium containing closely spaced discs was suddenly brought into rotation. The discs accelerated the helium until a steady state was reached. By measuring the

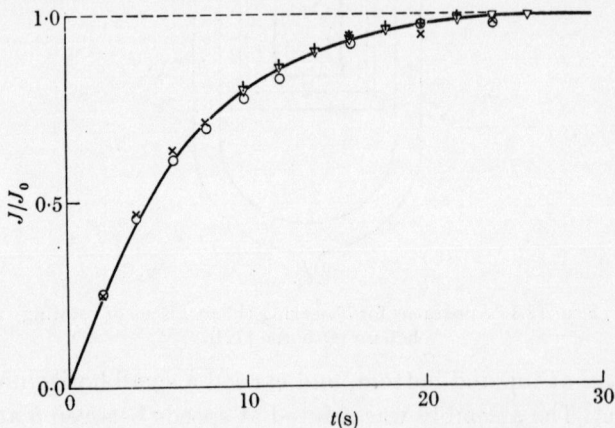

FIG. 12.2. The angular momentum J of a bucket of liquid helium, as a function of the time t after the start of rotation of the bucket at a speed of 0.78_5 rad s^{-1}. The value J_0 corresponds to complete rotation of the whole fluid (Hall [73]).

torque on the system and integrating over the time, Hall obtained the total angular momentum imparted to the liquid. The experiment was performed at a temperature of about 1·27 K, where $\rho_n \simeq 0.04\rho$, and $\rho_s \simeq 0.96\rho$. Hence if both the normal and superfluids rotate, the imparted angular momentum will be about 24 times greater than if only the normal fluid rotates.

Fig. 12.2 shows values derived for J, the angular momentum of the system, as a function of the time of rotation at an angular velocity of 0·78 rad s^{-1}. We see that after about 20 seconds the angular momentum rises to a value J_0 corresponding to complete rotation of the whole fluid.

12.2. The two-fluid model in rotating helium

The experiments described in the previous section show that the whole mass of liquid helium II may be set into a state of uniform rotation. Hence the condition curl $\mathbf{v}_s = 0$, which we have hitherto taken as part of the two-fluid model, cannot be generally valid. Yet other experiments show that the fountain pressure and the velocity of second sound are unchanged by

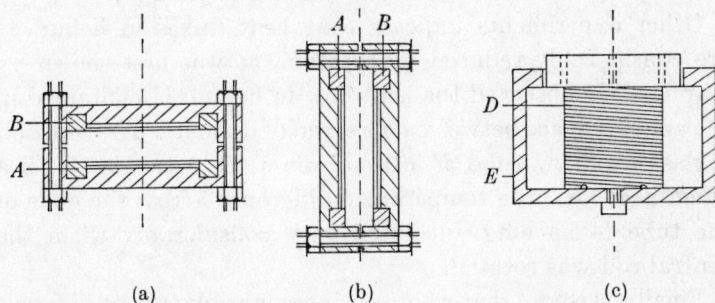

FIG. 12.3. Resonators used to observe the propagation of second sound in rotating helium. The axes of rotation are vertical. (a) and (b) show two orientations of an axial mode resonator and (c) a radial mode resonator. For further details see text (after Hall and Vinen [74]).

rotation, so there must still be a clear distinction between the normal and superfluids.

An informative experiment is due to Hall and Vinen. These authors measured the velocity and attenuation of second sound in rotating helium using the resonators shown in Fig. 12.3. The resonator in Fig. 12.3(a) is circularly symmetrical about the vertical axis of rotation, and acts as a half-wave resonant cavity in which the second sound propagates parallel to the axis of symmetry. The heater generating the second sound is wound to and fro between slots in the ring A, and the phosphor bronze thermometer used as a detector is wound on ring B. The resonator in Fig. 12.3(b) is similar, but mounted so that the sound propagates perpendicularly to the axis of rotation. The third resonator (Fig. 12.3(c)) is a radial mode cavity, consisting of the annular space between an ebonite cylinder D

9

and a brass outer case E. The resistance wires forming the heater and thermometer are wound on the cylinder D.

The amplitude of the signal in cavity 12.3(a) was apparently unchanged by steady rotations of the order of a few radians per second, but the signals in the other two cavities were appreciably reduced. The extra attenuation was a function of temperature, and *directly proportional to the speed of rotation*. In addition the coefficient of attenuation for a given velocity and temperature appeared to be the same for cavities (b) and (c).

Other experiments indicate that heat fluxes in helium II are considerably reduced by rotation, as was first shown by Kapitza. He observed the heat flow in helium II contained in the annular space between a glass rod of diameter 0·50 mm and a glass capillary tube of internal diameter 0·62 mm. With a given heat flux, the temperature difference across the ends of the tube (4 cm long) increased very considerably when the central rod was rotated.

Finally, we note that whatever is responsible for the different behaviour of rotating helium, it does not seem to be a change in the nature of the thermal excitations. Thus Woods has measured the distribution of monochromatic neutrons scattered from a small bucket of helium $2\frac{1}{4}$ inches in diameter. There was no discernable difference between the results for the bucket at rest and for a rotation of 60 rev min^{-1}. Hence we conclude that the excitation spectrum (section 7.3) is unchanged by the rotation.

12.3. Oscillating discs in rotating helium

One might account for the results of the previous two sections by postulating a weak frictional force acting between the normal and superfluids. In this case the superfluid in a rotating vessel would eventually be dragged round by the normal component. However, other experiments show that the actual situation is more complex.

Andronikashvili measured the density of the normal fluid by observing the period of oscillation of a pile of discs suspended in liquid helium (section 6.5). The discs were positioned close together so that all the normal fluid between them was set into oscillation. On the other hand the superfluid appeared to be at rest. In a variant of this experiment due to Hall, a similar pile of discs was allowed to oscillate in a vessel of uniformly rotating helium.

When measurements were made in liquid helium I the period of oscillation of the discs was unaffected by an imposed steady rotation, as might be expected. However, below the lambda point, unusual effects were observed. The experiments were mostly carried out at as low a temperature as possible (1·27 K), so that the helium between the discs was nearly all superfluid, $\rho_s \simeq 0\cdot96\rho$. It was then apparent that the angular frequency of oscillation Ω varied with the angular velocity of steady rotation ω_0. Hall displayed the effect of this rotation on Ω in terms of an effective density ρ'. That is, he assumed that the change in period could be described in terms of an increase ρ' in the density of the helium dragged round between the discs.

Fig. 12.4 shows results obtained using an apparatus with rough discs, and we see two striking features. For some frequencies of rotation and oscillation, the additional density ρ' is *negative*. This result is quite inexplicable in terms of the

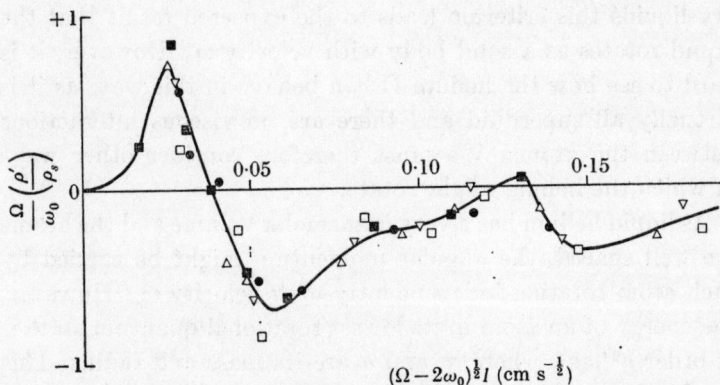

FIG. 12.4. The quantity ρ' deduced from Hall's oscillating disc experiments with relatively slow rotation and rough surfaces; for details see text. Open points for a period of about 3 s: $\square$, $\omega_0 = 0\cdot140$; $\triangledown$, $\omega_0 = 0\cdot196$; $\triangle$, $\omega_0 = 0\cdot275$. Solid points for period of about 7 s: $\bullet$, $\omega_0 = 0\cdot098$; $\blacksquare$, $\omega_0 = 0\cdot140$ rad s^{-1} (Hall [75]).

normal fluid dragging some of the superfluid into motion. The value of ρ' also appears to vary periodically with l, the spacing between the discs, another result we would not expect to follow from an ordinary frictional force acting between the two fluids. We discuss this experiment again in section 13.3.

12.4. Vortex lines

We now ask how the nature of liquid helium II is modified by rotation. Let us consider a cylindrical vessel of helium II, rotating at constant angular velocity ω, at so low a temperature that there is hardly any normal fluid, and we may ignore any distinction between the two densities ρ_s and ρ. For the same reason we will also ignore the distinction between the internal energy U and free energy F. We have seen that the helium has the normal angular momentum of an ordinary liquid, how then does the liquid helium behave so as to have the lowest energy characteristic of thermal equilibrium?

The usual condition for equilibrium in a system within a closed vessel rotating with a constant angular velocity $\boldsymbol{\omega_0}$ is obtained by minimizing the quantity $(U - \mathbf{I} \cdot \boldsymbol{\omega_0})$, where U is the internal energy and $\mathbf{I}$ the total angular momentum of the system (see, for example Landau and Lifshitz [76]). For ordinary liquids this criterion leads to the expected result that the liquid rotates as a solid body with velocity $\boldsymbol{\omega_0}$. However, it is hard to see how the helium II can behave in this way, as it is virtually all superfluid and there are no viscous interactions between the atoms. We must therefore consider other ways in which the helium might rotate.

As liquid helium has a very large molar volume and the atoms are well spaced, the angular momentum might be carried by each atom rotating independently with velocity $\boldsymbol{\omega_0}$. However, the energy of an atom in its lowest rotational quantum state is of order $\hbar^2/ma^2$, where m and a are its mass and radius. This is of order 10^{-16} ergs, which is comparable with the thermal energy of the atom! Moreover, the wave function of a helium atom is spherically symmetric, so it is hard to see that the concept of rotation has any significance.

The experiments of section 12.1 show that the whole mass of liquid helium II in a simply connected region may be set into a state of rotation. Hence the condition curl $\mathbf{v}_s = 0$, used in the two-fluid model to ensure the absence of viscosity in the superfluid, cannot be generally valid. Therefore several authors have developed the hypothesis that rotating helium is threaded by an array of vortex lines, as originally suggested by H. London and Onsager. Such vortex lines permit the liquid to have the angular momentum appropriate to solid body rotation, at the expense of a very small increase in the energy, while maintaining the condition curl $\mathbf{v}_s = 0$ over almost the whole volume.

To form some physical picture, we think of a vortex line by considering a two-dimensional velocity field in a perfect fluid surrounding a long straight cylinder, such that

$$v = A/r, \tag{12.4}$$

where v is the (tangential) velocity at a distance r from the centre of the cylinder, and A is a constant. If we now shrink the cylinder to a suitable size, we may remove it, leaving a vortex whose sides are held back by the centrifugal forces. Except where the liquid is threaded by a hole, the velocity (12.4) is everywhere irrotational (curl $\mathbf{v} = 0$), yet the liquid has considerable angular momentum. We define the strength of the vortex line by its circulation

$$\kappa = \oint \mathbf{v} \cdot d\mathbf{l} \tag{12.5}$$

where the integral is taken round any path enclosing the vortex.

The determination of the most stable arrangement of vortex lines in a vessel of uniformly rotating helium is a matter of some difficulty. However, it appears that for not too low speeds of rotation, the liquid will be threaded by a uniform array of similar lines each with circulation κ. In order to simulate solid body rotation with angular velocity ω_0, the circulation round any circular path of radius r concentric with the axis of rotation must be equal to $2\pi r^2 \omega_0$. However, this total circulation is also equal to $(\pi r^2) n_0 \kappa$, where n_0 is the number of lines per unit area. Hence the density of lines needed to simulate solid body rotation is

$$n_0 = 2\omega_0/\kappa. \tag{12.6}$$

As we discuss in section 12.5, there are reasons for supposing that κ takes the value h/m; in this case, for an angular velocity of 1 rad s^{-1}, n_0 is approximately 2000, corresponding to a spacing between lines of about 0·2 mm.

Finally, we make a rough estimate of a_0, the radius of the central core of a vortex, by balancing the force due to the surface tension T against the Bernouilli force, viz.

$$\frac{2T}{a_0} = \tfrac{1}{2}\rho v^2 = \tfrac{1}{2}\rho\left(\frac{\kappa}{2\pi a_0}\right)^2;$$

hence again taking $\kappa = h/m$,

$$a_0 = \frac{\rho\kappa^2}{16\pi^2 T} \simeq 0\cdot3 \text{ Å}.$$

Thus we expect no hole in the liquid, but rather a narrow region where the wave function tends to zero. The exact value of the energy parameter a_0 can only be found if we have a good wave function for the core, but it will clearly be of atomic dimensions.

12.5. The quantization of circulation

To obtain a complete description of a vortex line we need to specify its wave function. In the region of its core this is a very difficult problem which has not yet been solved. However, we can describe the irrotational flow pattern outside the core with Feynman's wave functions introduced in section 11.7. In this case it follows that the circulation round a vortex line in helium II should be quantized (Feynman [70]).

Let us consider a system of helium at a sufficiently low temperature that we may ignore the excitations, so that its wave function is given by

$$\psi = \left\{\exp i \sum_i s(\mathbf{R}_i)\right\}\varphi, \tag{11.12}$$

where $\mathbf{R}_i$ specifies the position of the ith particle and $s(\mathbf{R}_i)$ is a function which changes steadily and smoothly with position. We now ask how this wave function changes if each atom in the ring of atoms shown in Fig. 12.5 moves a distance $\Delta \mathbf{R}_i$ into the position previously occupied by the $(i+1)$th atom. While making this rearrangement we temporarily displace such

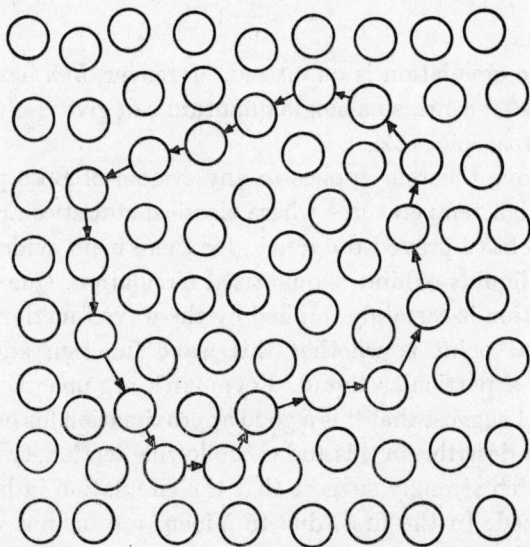

FIG. 12.5. A displacement of each atom to the site of its neighbour in a ring is equivalent to a permutation of the atoms. For ⁴He atoms the wave function cannot change as the result of such a displacement (Feynman [70]).

adjacent atoms as may be necessary in order to give a clear passage to the atoms in the ring. On account of the term φ, the wave function never falls to zero, so there are then no hidden changes of the sign in ψ during the displacement. Hence as all the atoms move one place round the ring, the phase must change by an amount

$$\sum_{\text{ring}} \{\operatorname{grad} s(\mathbf{R}_i)\} \cdot \Delta \mathbf{R}_i \, .$$

According to (11.13) $\operatorname{grad} s(\mathbf{R}_i) = (m/\hbar)\mathbf{v}_s(\mathbf{R})$, so that the change of phase is

$$\sum_{\text{ring}} = (m/\hbar)\mathbf{v}_s(\mathbf{R}) \cdot \Delta \mathbf{R} = (m/\hbar)\kappa,$$

where κ is the circulation round the ring. As we are dealing with an assembly of Bose particles, the final state of the helium, in which each atom has taken the place of its neighbour, is indistinguishable from the initial state. Therefore the phase change must be zero or an integral multiple, n, of 2π. Hence

$$\kappa = \frac{nh}{m} ;$$

that is the circulation is quantized. Moreover, h/m has a value of about 10^{-3} c.g.s., so a single quantum can give rise to effects on a macroscopic scale.

The above theorem applies to any system of Bose particles, even at high temperatures where classical statistics apply. We appear to have proved too much, for there is no evidence that ordinary liquids exhibit a quantized circulation. Quantization of circulation is certainly implied by the wave function (11.12), the crucial point is whether this wave function adequately describes a particular liquid. Feynman's arguments given in Chapter 11 suggest that it is a good approximation for helium II.

We now describe, in this and the following section, two experiments which strongly suggest that the circulation in helium II is quantized. In the first, due to Vinen, the helium was contained within a metal tube, along the axis of which was stretched a fine metal wire (5 cm long and 0·001 inches diameter). For a perfectly uniform wire, in the absence of circulation, the modes of vibration of the wire are doubly degenerate, as it can vibrate independently in two perpendicular directions. However, any circulation κ round the wire removes the degeneracy, and the wire vibrates in two circularly polarized modes differing in frequency by an amount

$$\Delta f = \rho_s \kappa / 2\pi W,$$

where W is the sum of the mass per unit length of the wire and half the mass of liquid displaced by this length. The experiment consists in setting the helium into rotation and measuring the frequency splitting Δf.

Vinen found that some of his readings changed if the wire was vibrated very strongly, probably because a vortex line was only partly, and therefore unstably, connected to the wire. The values of all the stable readings are plotted in Fig. 12.6 as a histogram, and we see that most of the points correspond to a circulation of either zero or approximately h/m. This result has been confirmed in similar experiments by Whitmore and Zimmermann who also observed circulations of $2h/m$ and $3h/m$.

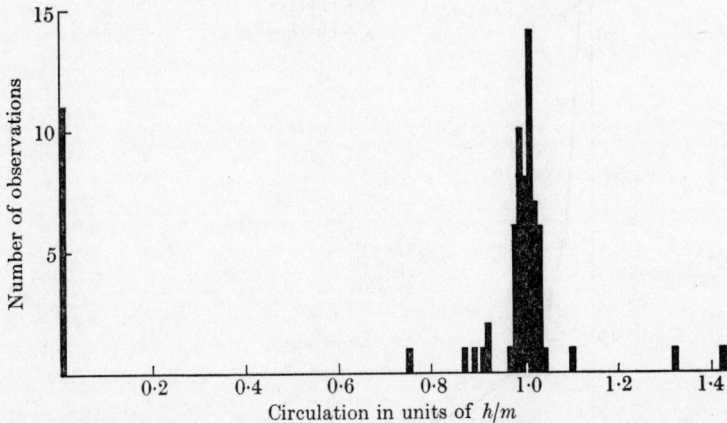

FIG. 12.6. Histogram showing the values of the circulation in Vinen's experiment which were stable against repeated vibration of the wire at large amplitude (Vinen [77]).

A notable feature of Vinen's experiment is that he observed the circulation to persist round the wire for several hours, and apparently indefinitely, after the cylindrical vessel containing the helium had been brought to rest. That is, a *persistent current* of circulating liquid can be set up in helium II analogous to a persistent current in a superconductor (see also reference [78]). Finally we note that, as the circulation is quantized, a vortex motion must have a certain minimum energy. Therefore we might expect that at sufficiently low speeds of rotation, no quanta will be excited, and the superfluid will remain at rest. This effect has been demonstrated by Hess and Fairbank [79], but the critical speed is so extremely low that we may generally assume that rotation always produces vortices.

12.6. Ions and vortices

In section 10.5 we described studies of the motion of ions in liquid helium II under the action of an electric field. In general the ions are scattered by the thermal excitations, so it is necessary to apply an electric field in order to maintain a

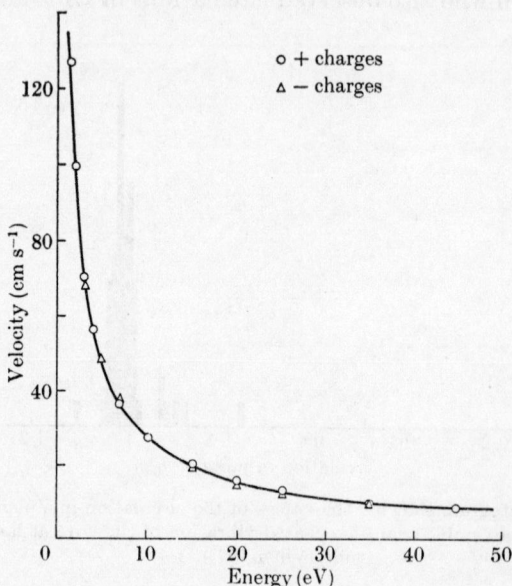

FIG. 12.7. The velocity of positive and negative ions in liquid helium measured as a function of their energy. The full line shows the theoretical values calculated from equations (12.7) and (12.8), by assuming that the ion carries one quantum of circulation and has a core radius of 1·2 Å (Rayfield and Reif [80]).

uniform drift velocity. We now describe an experiment by Rayfield and Reif, using rather higher fields, at temperatures down to 0·3 K, where there are hardly any excitations to cause scattering. The ions then move very much as free particles with no retarding resistance.

Figure 12.7 shows the velocities of these ions as a function of the accelerating voltage V. The results show two remarkable features. The velocities are very much lower (order of 10 cm s^{-1}) than those observed in the experiments of section 10.5 (order of 10^3 cm s^{-1}). Moreover, the velocity of the ions *decreases* with increasing energy, a result at first sight so improbable that the authors describe confirmatory experiments with different electrode arrangements. They conclude from the very low velocities that the carriers of the electric charge are quite different entities from those in the high-temperature experiments; they must be much more massive. Moreover they travel more slowly as their energy increases! Rayfield and Reif point out that this unusual behaviour may be accounted for if the charge carriers are vortex rings.

According to classical hydrodynamics, the energy and velocity of a vortex ring of radius r and circulation κ in a fluid of density ρ are given by

$$E = \tfrac{1}{2}\rho\kappa^2 r(\eta - \tfrac{7}{4}) \tag{12.7}$$
$$v = \kappa/4\pi r(\eta - \tfrac{1}{4}), \tag{12.8}$$

where

$$\eta = \ln(8r/a_0)$$

and a_0 is the radius of the core; note that η depends only weakly on r. It then follows from (12.7) and (12.8) that the velocity v of a vortex ring with circulation κ and energy E varies approximately as $1/E$, in accord with the experimental results. The exact relation between E and v depends on the two parameters κ and a_0. The authors therefore proceed by taking κ to have its quantized value h/m, and then choose a_0 to give the best fit to the experimental points. The best value comes out to be $a_0 = 1\cdot2$ Å, and this leads to the theoretical curve shown in Fig. 12.7, which is in excellent agreement with the experimental points. Thus the experiment gives support to (a) the existence of vortex rings in helium II, (b) the fact that their circulation is close to the quantum value of h/m, and (c) a value of the parameter of a_0 close to $1\cdot2$ Å.

CHAPTER XIII

VORTEX LINES IN HELIUM II

THE experiments of the last chapter suggest that a vessel of uniformly rotating helium II is threaded by an array of vortex lines. We now outline some properties of helium associated with the presence of these lines, and then discuss other experiments in which high velocities of the normal and superfluids produce a state of *turbulence*, in which the liquid is threaded by an irregular tangled mass of vortex lines. We begin by considering the appropriate density to be associated with the vortex motion.

13.1. Vortex lines and excitations

So far, we have only considered the rotation of helium II at temperatures close to 1 K where there is little distinction between the density of the superfluid and that of the actual liquid. We must now ask how the presence of thermal excitations affects the vortex lines.

It is often stated that at the higher temperatures the vortex lines are disturbances in the superfluid. Although this may be a convenient shorthand for expressing the true position, it is also a misleading one. The vortex motions at all temperatures are essentially motions of helium atoms in the real liquid. However, except at temperature zero, we have to consider the effect of the thermal excitations on this vortex motion. Following the method of section 8.4, we fix our attention on a small element of volume in some liquid helium at temperature zero. Due to the vortex motions this element will have a certain velocity, say $\mathbf{v_s}$. We next raise the temperature so as to create a number of thermal excitations on which we impose a drift velocity $\mathbf{v_n}$. Then, as shown in section 8.4, the momentum of the volume element may be written as $\rho_n \mathbf{v_n} + \rho_s \mathbf{v_s}$, where ρ_n and ρ_s are the densities of the normal and superfluids. That is, the density associated with the velocity field $\mathbf{v_s}$ is no longer ρ but ρ_s. To this extent the vortex is 'in the superfluid', but it is hard to form a physical picture.

The need to associate the superfluid density ρ_s with the vortex motion, rather than the total density ρ, is confirmed by experiments on the angular momentum of a vessel of rotating helium [81], and particularly of a gyroscope filled with the liquid [82, 83]. In one of these experiments the angular momentum of the helium in the gyroscope, itself immersed in a temperature bath of liquid helium, was sensed by applying a small torque to the system magnetically, and observing the tilt of the gyroscope. The helium in the gyroscope was set into rotation above the lambda point, then cooled to some temperature below the lambda point, and the angular momentum deduced from the observed tilts of up to 10°. Then, without any further rotation of the system, the temperature of the cryostat was raised, and measurements made at other temperatures. The results given in Fig. 13.1 show that the angular momentum

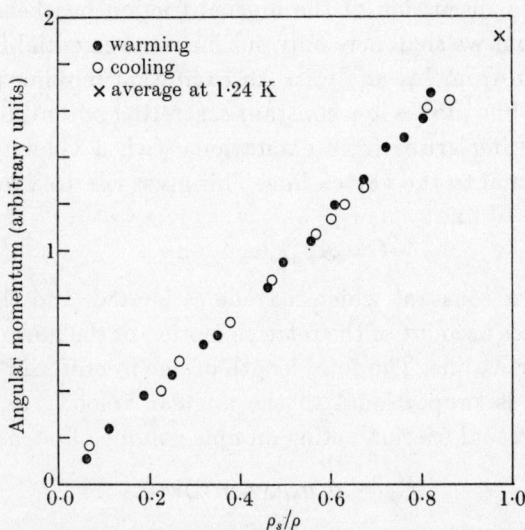

FIG. 13.1. Each point shows the angular momentum of persistent currents in liquid helium at a particular temperature, plotted against the values of ρ_s/ρ appropriate to that temperature (Mehl and Zimmermann [83]).

varied directly as the superfluid density as the temperature in one particular experiment was raised from 1·24 K towards the lambda point, and then reduced again. Note that although the angular velocity of the gyroscope was changed solely by altering the temperature, conservation of angular momentum is not violated, because angular momentum could be exchanged with the helium in the temperature bath. Under the circumstances of these experiments, it is the circulation of the helium in the gyroscope which is conserved, not its angular momentum.

13.2. Mutual friction

The core of a vortex is a very non-uniform region, and will therefore scatter the thermal excitations, i.e. the normal fluid. Hence, any motion of the normal fluid relative to a vortex line results in a force between the line and the fluid. The sums of these forces per unit volume give the so-called mutual friction F_{ns} between the normal and superfluids. It is this mutual friction term which is responsible for the attentuation of second sound in rotating helium described in section 12.2.

A detailed discussion of the mutual friction has been given by Vinen, but we shall here only outline some essential features that emerge from his analysis. An excitation moving parallel to a vortex line moves in a constant scattering potential, so the only scattering arises from excitations with a velocity component normal to the vortex line. This gives rise to a force per unit length of line

$$f = A\rho_n\rho_s(v_n - v_s),$$

where A is a constant which may be estimated, and the term $(v_n - v_s)$ takes account of the relative motion of the normal fluid and the vortex line. The total length of line in uniformly rotating helium is proportional to the angular velocity ω_0, hence the total mutual friction acting on unit volume of normal fluid

$$F_{ns} = A'\rho_n\rho_s(v_n - v_s)\omega_0, \tag{13.1}$$

where A' is another constant.

Given equation (13.1) it follows from the equations of motion that there is an additional attenuation of second sound of the form $\alpha' = A'\rho\omega_0/2c_2$, where c_2 is the velocity of the sound. That is, there is an additional attenuation of the sound proportional to the angular velocity of rotation, as is observed. Moreover we expect the attenuation to be very small when the second sound is propagating parallel to the axis (i.e. when $\mathbf{v}_n - \mathbf{v}_s$ is parallel to the vortex lines), and to be the same for all directions of propagation perpendicular to the axis. This is, in fact, the symmetry observed in the experiments. It is difficult to calculate the constant A' precisely, but its value turns out to have the correct order of magnitude.

13.3. Vortex waves

The mutual friction force of the last section accounts for the attentuation of second sound in rotating helium, but we have already mentioned that it will not account for the unusual effects observed when a pile of discs are oscillated in the rotating liquid (section 12.3). Before discussing this experiment, we describe another experiment in which the resonance effect suggested in Fig. 12.4 is shown even more clearly.

A single disc, roughened on its upper surface, was suspended on a torsion fibre, and oscillated a short distance below the surface of a bath of helium (Fig. 13.2). As time went on, the level of the liquid in the beaker slowly rose, because of film flow from the outer vessel, and the period of oscillation varied as shown in Fig. 13.3.

This experiment and that described in section 12.3 are readily interpreted in terms of waves on vortex lines, as originally discussed by Lord Rayleigh in connection with ordinary liquids. As a vortex line has an energy per unit length, it will tend to reduce its length to lower its energy, that is it appears to have a line tension. Hence if the vortex line is displaced in

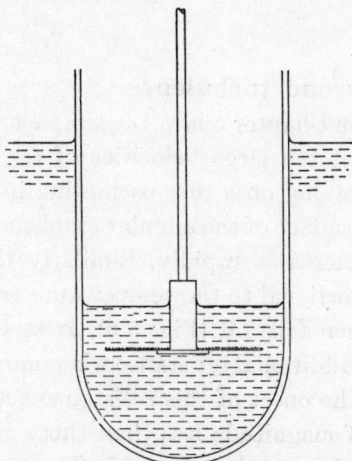

FIG. 13.2. Hall's single disc apparatus. The beaker surrounding the disc is rigidly connected to the torsion head from which the disc is suspended, and rotates with it (Hall [84]).

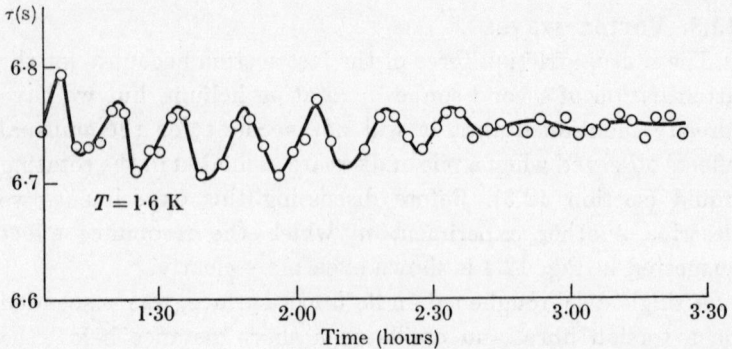

FIG. 13.3. The period τ of the disc of Fig. 13.2 oscillating in rotating liquid helium as a function of time (or of the changing level of the liquid). $\omega_0 = 0{\cdot}140$ rad s^{-1} (Hall [84]).

the liquid, so as to bow it out, the line tension will tend to return it to its equilibrium position. We thus have the necessary conditions for the line to support oscillations or vortex waves. In fact, the variations of frequency shown in Fig. 13.3 occur as the lengths of vortex line attached to the rough upper surface of the disc pass through resonant lengths for vortex waves. The results shown in Figs. 12.4 and 13.3, and of other similar experiments, can be satisfactorily explained in terms of this theory.

13.4. Heat flow and turbulence

We described in Chapter 5 how the simple two-fluid model is only valid for not too large velocities of the two fluids. For example, the damping on a disc oscillating in helium II (Fig. 5.2) is only independent of the angular amplitude until a certain value, when it increases rapidly. Similarly the heat flow in helium II is proportional to the temperature gradient for small gradients, but then falls off (Fig. 5.6). It seems that the two fluids experience additional resistance when moving at relatively high velocities. The onset of this resistance occurs at a *critical velocity*, orders of magnitude less than those given by Landau for the creation of thermal excitations. The rest of the chapter deals with the behaviour of the liquid in this *supracritical* region.

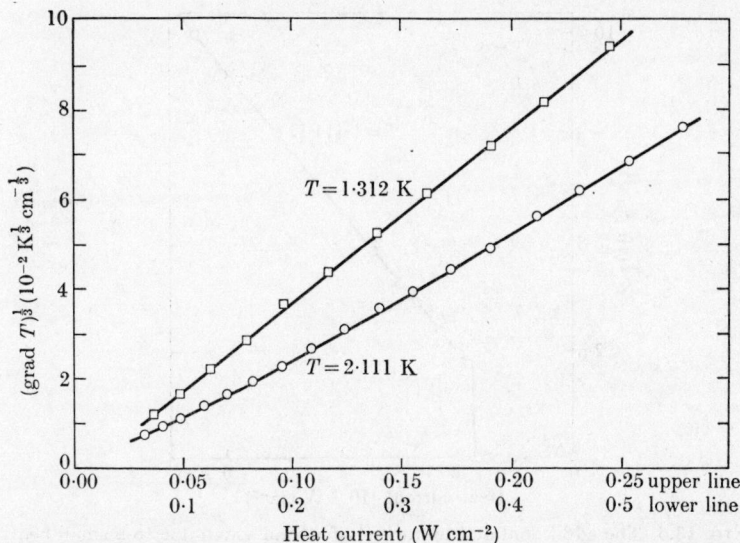

FIG. 13.4. The heat current in liquid helium in a tube of large cross-section ($2 \cdot 40 \times 6 \cdot 45$ mm) plotted against the cube root of the temperature gradient (Vinen [85]).

The transition to the supracritical region is usually quite abrupt, as shown by the measurements of Fig. 5.7. We see that the extra resistance soon exceeds the initial value in the linear region. The heat flow then varies approximately as the cube root of the temperature gradient, as shown in Fig. 13.4. This additional resistance is not observed immediately on passing a heat flux through the liquid, but takes a few seconds to build up. Vinen studied this transition by passing a heat current transversely through waves of second sound generated in a resonator, and observing the amplitude of the second sound as a function of the heat current. He found that small heat flows made no difference to the amplitude of the second sound, but on exceeding a critical value, the attenuation of the second sound built up to an additional value roughly proportional to the square of the heat flux (Fig. 13.5).

The build-up times observed by Vinen were always reproducible provided that the liquid had been rested for several minutes prior to the measurement. However, observations of

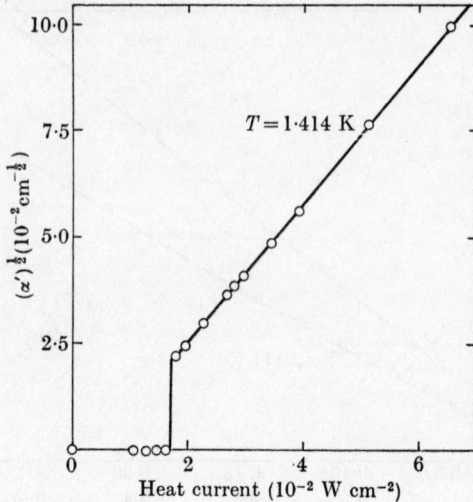

FIG. 13.5. The additional attenuation α' of second sound due to a small heat current (Vinen [85]).

the second sound made a few seconds after switching off the heat current showed that the liquid was still disturbed. Hence, on switching on the heat current again, the thermal resistance and attenuation built up more quickly. Other authors have studied the temperature gradients in long capillaries filled with helium II. When the critical velocity is exceeded, the transition to the supracritical region is observed as a region of higher thermal resistance spreading out from one or more points on the tube. All these results are reminiscent of the behaviour of turbulence in ordinary liquids, and suggest that some form of turbulence is being created in the helium.

The turbulence impedes the flow of the normal fluid and hence gives rise to an additional thermal resistance. A qualitative analysis of this effect has been given by Vinen who assumes reasonably enough that the turbulent state is both homogeneous and isotropic. In addition, the growth of turbulence at any instant is assumed to depend only on the present state of the helium and not on its previous condition. In this case the rate of increase of L, the length of vortex line per unit volume, can only depend on f, the force on unit length of line, and on ρ_s and κ. From dimensional considerations it follows that

$$\frac{\mathrm{d}L}{\mathrm{d}t} = \kappa L^2 \varphi\left(\frac{f}{\rho_s \kappa^2 L^{\frac{1}{2}}}\right),$$

where φ is some function. The equilibrium value of L for a given value of f is specified by the condition $(\mathrm{d}L/\mathrm{d}t) = 0$, that is, $\varphi = 0$. Hence

$$L_0^{\frac{1}{2}} \propto f/\rho_s \kappa^2,$$

where L_0 is the equilibrium value of L.

The force f arises from the interactions between the excitations and the cores of the vortices, and as discussed in section 13.2 is proportional to the relative velocity $(v_n - v_s)$. Hence

$$L_0 \propto (v_n - v_s)^2.$$

The total force maintaining the equilibrium length L_0 of vortex line is proportional to L_0 and to $(v_n - v_s)$, hence the retarding force on the normal fluid

$$F_{ns} \propto (v_n - v_s)^3.$$

It then follows from an extension of the equations of motion in section 6.2 that, when this resistance predominates, the heat flow varies as the cube root of the temperature gradient, in agreement with the results of Fig. 13.4.

CHAPTER XIV

CRITICAL VELOCITIES

WE have seen in the previous chapter that the turbulent state may be described in terms of a mass of vortex line, whose total length increases with the increasing relative velocity of the two fluids. We have yet to enquire how this length of line is originally created in the ideal superfluid state. In particular, we have to calculate the values of the critical velocities observed in different kinds of experiments. This problem is by no means solved, but we now indicate a few of the principal features which must be considered.

We have already shown in section 8.1 that superfluidity is only possible if motion of the liquid does not generate thermal excitations. The Landau criterion, equation (8.4), sets an upper limit for flow without any generation of excitations, of about

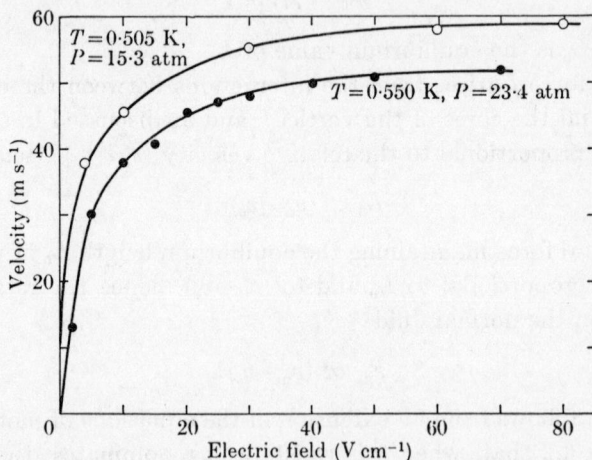

FIG. 14.1. The drift velocity of negative ions in helium II under pressure, as a function of the applied electric field (Meyer and Reif [86]).

60 m s^{-1}. However, the onset of turbulence generally destroys superfluidity long before this velocity is reached, as in the experiments on heat flow and viscosity described in the previous chapters. Indeed, there appears to be only one set of experiments which show a limiting velocity of the order of 60 m s^{-1}. Fig. 14.1 shows the velocity of negative ions in helium II as a function of an applied electric field. At relatively low fields, the velocity of the ions is limited by the scattering of the thermal excitations, but increases steadily with increasing field. However, at higher fields, the velocity approaches a constant value which is close to the Landau criterion for the formation of rotons in helium of the given densities. It therefore appears that in this region the velocity is limited by the generation of rotons.

14.1. v_s, v_n, or $v_n - v_s$?

Hitherto we have referred to critical velocities without clearly specifying which particular velocity of the two-fluid model is involved. If we consider a transition to turbulence from the linear region of the two-fluid model, then there are three velocities to consider: v_n, v_s, and $(v_n - v_s)$. As the supracritical

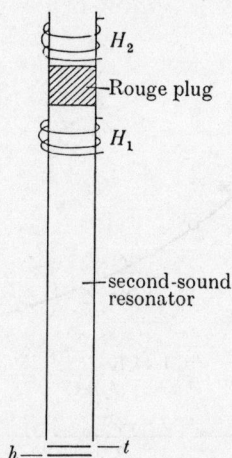

FIG. 14.2. Schematic diagram of the apparatus used in the heat flow experiments of Peshkov and Stryukov [87]).

condition consists of turbulence in the superfluid, the velocity v_s must be involved. We now describe an experiment which suggests that the velocity which determines the onset of turbulence is v_s rather than $(v_n - v_s)$.

Fig. 14.2 shows the apparatus used by Peshkov and Stryukov. A tube of helium 3·8 mm in diameter acts as a resonator for second sound generated by a heater h, and detected by a thermometer t. The plug of packed rouge acts as a superleak, below and above which are heaters H_1 and H_2. The authors' procedure was as follows. First the heater H_1 was switched on so as to give a heat flux W_1 well in the turbulent region (by a factor ~ 8). This caused turbulence to build up with a half-time τ, which was measured by observing the time taken for the second sound signal to fall to half its amplitude. The experiment was then repeated in the following way. The helium was allowed to return to its original condition, and a heat flux W_2 supplied by H_2 so as to induce a flow of superfluid through the tube with velocity v_s. (The rouge plug ensures that the normal fluid remains at rest.) The heat flux W_1 was then switched on as before, and the time constant τ measured again. Finally this procedure was repeated for a range of values of W_2, that is, of v_s.

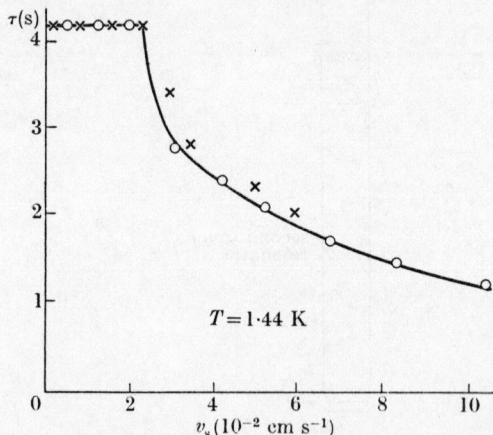

FIG. 14.3. The relaxation time for the establishment of turbulent conditions as measured by Peshkov and Stryukov; for details see text. v_s is the initial velocity of the superfluid. The points ○ are for the case when the normal fluid in the resonator was initially at rest, and the points ✗ for an initial counterflow of both normal and superfluid (Peshkov and Stryukov [87]).

The results (Fig. 14.3) show that τ was reduced by high initial values of v_s. Apparently these high values created some turbulence before the flux W_1 was switched on, so that the final turbulence (due to W_1) took less time to build up. The critical velocity is given by the break in the curve. The whole experiment was then repeated in a rather different way:

(1) A relatively small heat flux w_1 *somewhat less than the critical value* was generated in H_1, so as to induce a counter-current flow of both normal and superfluids in the tube.

(2) After equilibrium had been established, the energy to the heater was increased to the large supracritical value W_1.

(3) The time τ was now measured as a function of w_1. These times are also shown in Fig. 14.3 plotted against the values of v_s produced by w_1; the change in τ sets in at the same values of v_s as previously. Hence, the onset of turbulence appears unaffected by the presence of a velocity $(v_n - v_s)$ which at the temperatures involved exceeded v_s by a factor of over ten.

14.2. Two critical velocities

Some experiments show two critical velocities. Fig. 14.4 shows the damping on a sphere oscillating in liquid helium II as a function of the maximum amplitude (or velocity) of the oscillation. At low amplitudes, region A, the damping has a constant value equal to that we would associate with the normal viscosity η_n. At higher amplitudes there appear to be two critical velocities, at each of which the damping rises sharply. In the intermediate region C, the damping is independent of the amplitude, and is approximately what we would expect for an ordinary liquid of viscosity η_n and a density ρ equal to the total density of the helium. It appears that, above the transition at the lower amplitude, both fluids are coupled together by the mutual friction and move as one.

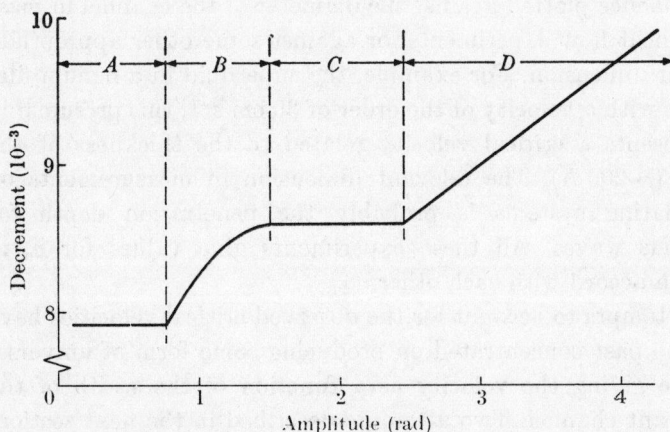

FIG. 14.4. The damping on a sphere oscillating in liquid helium at 2·149 K with a period of 18·5 s (after Donnelly and Hollis Hallett [88]).

The second transition in Fig. 14.4 appears to correspond, at least approximately, with the onset of turbulence in an ordinary classical liquid with a viscosity η_n and density ρ, equal to the density of the whole liquid. That is, the Reynolds numbers for these transitions are quite similar to those observed in experiments on liquid helium I. This result again suggests that, in the region C, the normal and superfluids are coupled together quite closely. For the rest of the chapter, however, we shall be concerned only with the first critical velocity which marks the boundary of the pure superfluid condition.

14.3. Measurements of the critical velocity

The transition to the turbulent state exhibits itself in a wide variety of experiments. In general the critical velocity in flow experiments *increases* as the diameter of the channel *decreases*. In addition the observed critical velocities may also depend somewhat on the temperature. We now collect together the results of various experiments exhibiting a critical velocity v_c, and in view of the dependence of v_c on temperature we restrict ourselves to one temperature, 1·4 K, so chosen because most authors quote values hereabout.

Fig. 14.5 shows the velocity of the superfluid at the onset of turbulence plotted against the diameter of the channel in mass and heat flow experiments, or against some other appropriate linear dimension. For example, the superfluid in a helium film flows with a velocity of the order of 30 cm s^{-1}; this presumably represents a critical velocity related to the thickness of the film ($\sim$200 Å). The relevant dimension in measurements on oscillating systems is probably the penetration depth for viscous waves. All these experiments give values for v_c in rough accord with each other.

Attempts to account for the observed critical velocities have in the past concentrated on producing some form of universal curve giving the velocity as a function of the width of the relevant channel. Two attempts described in the next section, based on criteria for the formation of vortices in the superfluid, lead to the dotted line shown in Fig. 14.5. The agreement with

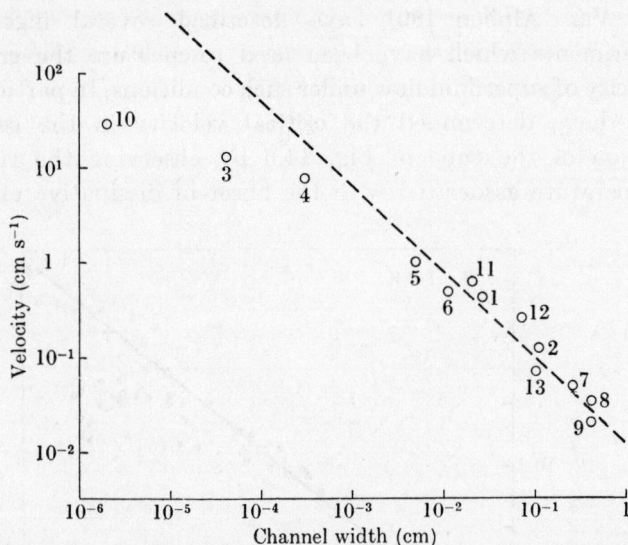

FIG. 14.5. The superfluid critical velocity v_c at a temperature of about 1·4 K as a function of channel size, measured in experiments on flow (1, 2), heat flow (3–6), second sound (7–9), film flow (10), oscillations (11, 12), and rotation viscometer (13). The dashed line shows the critical velocity given by equation (14.2).

experiment is only fair, and there are fundamental difficulties to the theory which we outline in the next section.

New information on critical velocities has recently been given by experiments of a type shown very schematically in Fig. 14.6. The plugs at A and B consist of tightly packed powder, so that if a hydrostatic pressure is applied across the ends of the tube XY, the only flow possible in the central region will be motion of the superfluid, as the normal fluid is 'clamped' between the two plugs. De Bruyn Ouboter, Taconis,

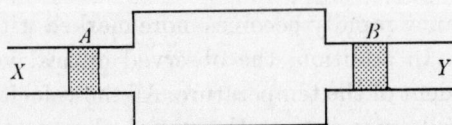

FIG. 14.6. Schematic diagram of apparatus to measure the critical velocity of superfluid flow when the normal fluid is clamped by constrictions at A and B; see text.

and Van Alphen [89] have described several ingenious experiments which have been used to measure the critical velocity of superfluid flow under such conditions. In particular, they have determined the critical velocity in the central portion of the tube of Fig. 14.6 by observing the rise of temperature associated with the onset of dissipative effects.

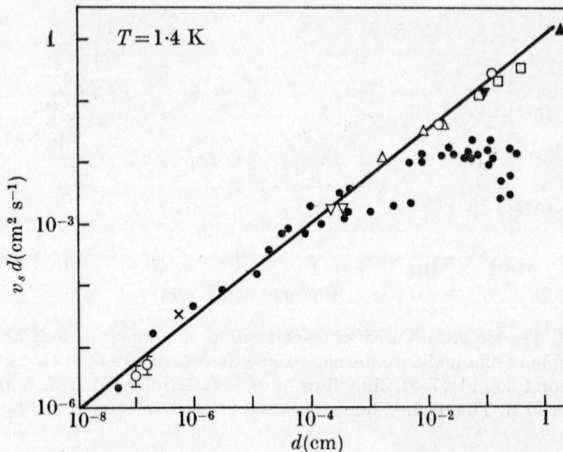

Fig. 14.7. The critical superfluid velocity v_s plotted as $v_s d$ versus d, where d is the width of the relevant channel. The small solid circles are earlier results such as those shown in Fig. 14.5. The larger symbols were obtained with the normal fluid 'clamped' by plugs. The straight lines show the relation $v_s \simeq 1/\sqrt[4]{d}$ cm s^{-1}. (De Bruyn Ouboter, Taconis, and Van Alphen [89].)

The results of such measurements are displayed in Fig. 14.7, which gives the product of critical velocity and channel width as a function of channel width.

Fig. 14.7 shows that, for channel sizes above about 1 μm in diameter, the critical velocities when the normal fluid is clamped are appreciably greater than those observed by other methods. This discrepancy rapidly becomes more marked with increasing channel size. In addition, the observed critical velocities are now independent of the temperature. All the velocities obtained in this way fall quite close to the straight line representing the relation $v_c \simeq 1/\sqrt[4]{d}$ cm s^{-1}, where d is the width of the channel.

The interpretation of these results is still not clear. De

Bruyn Ouboter *et al.* suggest that the lower values of the critical velocity observed previously correspond to ordinary classical turbulence in the normal fluid. These authors state that the criterion for the onset of this turbulence is the classical Reynold's number evaluated using the normal fluid velocity v_n, the normal viscosity η_n, and the total density $\rho = \rho_n + \rho_s$. They calculate that in heat flow experiments (where $v_s = (\rho_n/\rho_s)v_n$) the superfluid velocity when turbulence occurs *in the normal fluid* is similar to the lower values shown for wide channels in Fig. 14.7. However, at least two points remain unexplained. If we are dealing with counter-current heat flows, it is hard to see why the relevant density to insert in the Reynolds number is ρ rather than ρ_n. Secondly, the critical velocities of the superfluid deduced from all the previous isothermal flow and viscosity measurements fall into the same pattern as the heat flow measurements, even though for flow measurements $v_s = v_n$, in contrast to the quite different relation $v_s = (\rho_n/\rho_s)v_n$ for heat flow experiments.

14.4. Theories of the critical velocity

We begin by mentioning two theories of the critical velocity in capillaries. These treatments lead to expressions for the velocity which reproduce some of the main features of the experimental results in Fig. 14.5. Yet we prefer to regard these treatments rather as a basis for illustrating the difficulties of the situation.

Atkins supposed that the vorticity in a capillary is initiated in the form of a closed ring of vortex line of radius R. He then regarded the ring as a particular form of elementary excitation, and applied the Landau criterion for the critical velocity

$$v_c = \epsilon/p,$$

where ϵ is the energy of the excitation and p its momentum. In fact a vortex ring carries no momentum, and the quantity must be replaced by I, the integrated impulse needed to create a vortex in a liquid initially at rest, see reference [90]. The energy and impulse of a ring of radius r are given by classical hydrodynamics as

$$E = \tfrac{1}{2}\rho\kappa^2 r\left\{\ln\left(\frac{8r}{a_0}\right) - \frac{7}{4}\right\}$$

$$I = \pi\rho\kappa r^2,$$

where κ is the circulation and a_0 the radius of the core. Substituting ρ_s for ρ, and the quantum value of h/m for κ, it follows that

$$\frac{E}{I} = \frac{\hbar}{mr}\left\{\ln\left(\frac{8r}{a_0}\right) - \frac{7}{4}\right\}.$$

As the logarithmic term depends only weakly on r, the lowest value of E/I will be given approximately by the largest permitted value of r, hence

$$v_c \approx \frac{\hbar}{mr_{max}}\ln\left(\frac{1\cdot4 r_{max}}{a_0}\right). \tag{14.1}$$

A quite similar expression has been derived by Feynman, who considers a flow of helium from the end of a tube into a vessel of still liquid.

Expression (14.1) has the merit that it gives some explanation for the magnitude of the critical velocity and its dependence on channel size. The value of a_0 is not critical and we use the figure of $1\cdot2$ Å deduced by Rayfield and Reif (section 12.6). Then, assuming somewhat arbitrarily that the critical diameter of the ring $2r_{max}$ is half the width of the channel d, we find that

$$v_c \approx \frac{4\hbar}{md}\ln\left(\frac{d}{3a_0}\right), \tag{14.2}$$

The relation (14.2) is shown by the dashed line in Fig. 14.5. We see that the expression gives a fair account of the critical velocity in relatively wide channels, but not when the width falls below 1 μm. Moreover, it does not predict any variation of the critical velocity with temperature. A more fundamental difficulty is that expression (14.2) is derived by assuming that the vortex ring, when formed, is approximately as large as the diameter of the capillary. That is, it may be of the order of 1 mm in diameter. On the atomic scale, this is an enormous size, and it is hard to see how such a large co-operative motion can suddenly be initiated in the helium. A reasonable figure for the greatest diameter of a vortex ring which could be created instantaneously in the liquid is probably of the order of 10^{-6} cm, and this corresponds to a critical velocity of about 100 cm s^{-1}!

To resolve the last mentioned difficulty, Vinen [91] suggests that high velocities are only required to *create* vortices. Quite possibly, a few vortex lines may already be present in the liquid at the start of an experiment, perhaps in a metastable state. In this case, much smaller velocities of the superfluid might be sufficient to expand the lines and set up appreciable turbulence. This possibility is supported by experiments such as those described in section 14.1. The presence of a heat current *less than the critical value* results in a faster build-up of turbulence when a much larger supracritical heat flux is switched on. It seems that the initial subcritical heat flow creates some turbulence, which is then expanded by the supra-critical flow.

We now outline an argument due to Glaberson and Donnelly [92] which shows that the presence of metastable vortex lines can lead to critical velocities of the observed magnitude. Fig. 14.8(a) shows a length of vortex line in a tube of liquid helium II which is at rest. The tube is assumed to be sufficiently rough that the ends of the lines are effectively pinned to surface rugosities and cannot slide together. The vortex takes up the configuration of least energy, which in this case is a straight line between the two pinning points. If the helium in the tube flows with a velocity v, the line will tend to bow out as in Fig. 14.8(b).

If the fluid velocity is steadily increased, the radius of curvature of the line decreases to a value $l/2$, Fig. 14.8(c), and then increases again. The greatest velocity is needed to produce the maximum curvature; once this velocity has been exceeded, the line will continue to expand. Hence the growth of the line will be limited unless the velocity of the fluid exceeds a critical value, v_c, which will be equal in magnitude to the velocity v_0

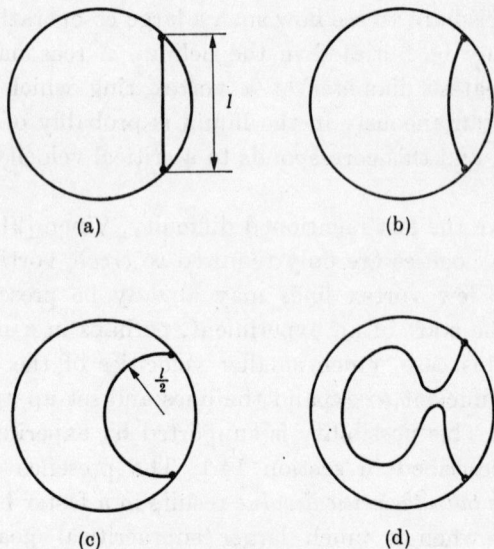

Fig. 14.8. Schematic diagram of a metastable vortex line; see text (Glaberson and Donnelly [92]).

associated with a vortex with the configuration of radius $l/2$ in Fig. 14.8(c). This velocity will be of the same order as (but less than) that for a closed ring of the same radius, hence, according to (12.8)

$$v_0 \sim \frac{\kappa}{2\pi l}\{\ln(4l/a_0) - \tfrac{1}{4}\},$$

where a_0 is the radius of the core. The lowest critical velocity occurs when $l \sim d$, the diameter of the tube, hence, remembering that $\kappa = h/m$, we find that

$$v_c \sim \frac{\hbar}{md}\{\ln(4d/a_0) - \tfrac{1}{4}\}, \qquad (14.3)$$

which is quite similar to (14.2),

Although equation (14.3) gives some account of the observed critical velocity, the model does not consider what happens to the vortex when the critical velocity has been exceeded. Perhaps some tangling process, like that shown in Fig. 14.8(d), results in the continuous generation of vortex rings. Finally, there remains the problem of how the initial vortex line is created. This may often arise fortuitously during the filling of the vessel. In fact, the only information under well defined conditions comes from experiments, similar to those in section 12.6, where vortex lines or rings are created by the motion of charged ions. Even here, however, the position is by no means clear, see for example reference [93], and further experiments are needed.

CHAPTER XV

MISCELLANEOUS ASPECTS OF LIQUID HELIUM II

WE now briefly review some other features of liquid helium II of particular interest.

15.1. The microscopic theory of liquid ^{4}He

Feynman's derivation of the excitation spectrum of liquid ^{4}He, described in Chapter 11, postulates the general form of the wave function, and then uses a variational method to obtain a more detailed expression. Many attempts have since been made to derive the energy spectrum directly, by solving a Schrödinger equation. It is comparatively simple to write down such an equation for the liquid, but very difficult to obtain a rigorous solution. There is now a large literature on this problem, and we shall do no more than indicate one or two salient features.

The essential step in deriving the energy spectrum from the Schrödinger equation was made by Bogoliubov [94] many years ago, in a rather difficult paper which was virtually ignored for several years. Bogoliubov considered a dilute gas of Bose particles *with weak interactions*. Because the particles obey Bose-Einstein statistics, nearly all the atoms are condensed in the ground state at temperatures close to zero. Hence the number of particles in the ground state is macroscopically large, and this permits certain approximations to be made. Bogoliubov was then able to solve the Schrödinger equation, written in terms of creation and destruction operators, by means of a suitable transformation. It turns out that the excitations of low wave number no longer have the usual particle type spectrum $\epsilon = p^2/2m$, but the spectrum $\epsilon = pc$, where c is the velocity of sound. Thus the presence of the interactions changes the low energy particle-like excitations into phonons! This result has since been confirmed by many other authors.

The ideas involved in Bogoliubov's treatment of a dilute Bose gas with interactions are somewhat unusual. Thus, the treatment implies that if we start with a perfect Bose gas in the ground state, and introduce interactions, then some atoms will be scattered out of the zero-momentum state. If we now introduce one *excitation* of low momentum p, there is a further increase in the number of atoms scattered out of the zero-momentum state. According to Brueckner and Sawada, the average number of these extra particles at any instant has the form

$$(\hbar/p)(\alpha Nm)^{\frac{1}{2}},$$

where N is the total number of atoms, m the atomic mass, and α a scattering parameter. Also, the fluctuation about this mean value is

$$(\sqrt{3}\hbar/2p)(\alpha Nm)^{\frac{1}{2}}.$$

Hence, for a low value of p, both the average number of extra particles excited out of the zero-momentum state, and the fluctuations in this number, will be large. The excited state bears little resemblance to a single-particle state. It is, in fact, a phonon state.

The systems considered above are all much less dense than real liquid helium, and do not reproduce the characteristic minimum in the phonon-roton excitation curve. Therefore attempts have been made to extend these treatments to higher densities with stronger interactions. In this case the so-called depletion effect becomes important. With stronger interactions,

more atoms are scattered out of the ground state, and Bogoliubov's approximation that virtually all the atoms are in the
ground state is no longer valid. This depletion of the ground
state may be quite large, and must be considered in any further
calculations. The backflow round a moving atom (section 11.5)
must also be taken into account, but we do not pursue these
points any further.

It is tempting to identify the condensed state, described
above, with the superfluid component of the two-fluid model.
Penrose has extended the work of Penrose and Onsager to
non-zero temperatures at which phonon excitations are present.
He is then able to identify the velocity v_s with the velocity of
the state into which the condensation occurs, but it is difficult
to form any physical picture of the situation. At very low
temperatures the density ρ_s of the superfluid in the two-fluid
model is almost equal to the full density ρ of the liquid. However, according to Penrose and Onsager the number of condensed atoms is only a fraction of the total, even at absolute
zero, where they estimate a figure of 8 per cent. Hence even if v_s
is the velocity of the ground state, ρ_s/ρ is clearly not the fraction
of atoms which are condensed, and we still have no physical
picture of the superfluid.

15.2. The Josephson effect in helium II

An important feature of one of the microscopic theories of
helium II has been pointed out by Richards and Anderson.
They stress the significance of Beliaev's result that the wave
function of the zero-momentum state in superfluid helium
contains a phase factor $\exp(-i\mu t/\hbar)$, where μ is the chemical
potential of an atom. They consider the experimental arrangement shown schematically in Fig. 15.1. Two baths of helium
standing at different levels are connected by a small orifice.
The chemical potentials of the helium at A and B will differ
by an amount mgz where m is the mass of the atom and z the
difference in hydrostatic level. Hence the phase of the helium
at A will slip with respect to the phase at B, at a rate $\omega =
mgz/\hbar$. Richards and Anderson suggest that this situation may

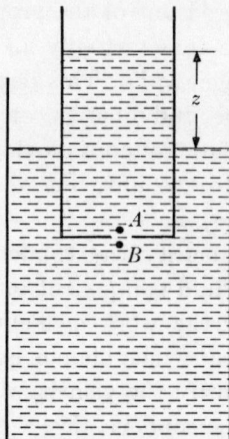

FIG. 15.1. Diagram to illustrate phase slip in liquid helium II (Richards and Anderson [95]); see text.

be stabilized by the motion of vortices either across, or away from, the orifice. As the phase change round a vortex of n quanta of circulation is $2n\pi$, the condition for stability might be

$$mgz/\hbar = v \,.\, 2n\pi$$

or

$$z = nh\nu/mg, \tag{15.1}$$

where ν is the rate at which vortices cross or leave the orifice.

Richards and Anderson sought to demonstrate this stability by introducing a transducer vibrating below the orifice at a frequency f, at an amplitude sufficient to induce turbulence in the liquid. The velocity field set up by the transducer lowers the level of the liquid in the central tube, both above and below the lambda point, in accord with the Pitot tube effect. Below the lambda point, however, the change in level appeared to occur in a series of steps. Taking ν as being equal to the frequency of the transducer, it seemed that the steps occurred at intervals of $(h\nu/mg)$. Although each step was not observed on every run, the experimental results certainly suggested a tendency towards such a spacing. (There is also a complication in that the vortices may be formed at a sub-multiple of the transducer frequency.) These results have since been confirmed by Khorana and Chandrasekhar [96], with particularly clear and well defined steps, about 1 mm high, in good numerical agreement with the value of hv/mg.

This striking experiment appears to be analogous to the a.c. Josephson effect in superconducting metals (see reference [21]). According to the above account, the steps arise because the system adjusts itself to balance the phase slip in accord with condition (15.1). That is, n takes up integral values appropriate to the level difference z. This result implies that the rate of the phase slip at the orifice determines the number of quanta of circulation in the vortex rings. These are remarkable effects, and further interesting experiments are to be expected, see for example Anderson [97].

15.3. The lambda transition

The regime of liquid helium II with its unusual kinetic properties sets in very abruptly at the lambda point, 2·17 K. We now briefly refer to experiments which throw some light on the nature of the transition which occurs at this temperature.

The first attempts to make measurements very close to the transition temperature were those on the specific heat by Fairbank, Buckingham, and Keller. In principle their method is quite simple; they supplied heat to a specimen of helium at a constant rate and observed the change of temperature. In fact, by taking various precautions, these authors attained a greater sensitivity than hitherto obtained in any specific heat measurements. This was done primarily by ensuring that thermal equilibrium was rapidly attained within the calorimeter, and that any heat leaks to the specimen were both small and regular.

The thermal relaxation time for a mass of liquid helium I may be very large, because it has a high thermal capacity and a very low thermal conductivity. The inside of the calorimeter therefore contained a system of copper fins, which ensured that none of the helium was further than 0·003 inches from a copper surface. In this way the relaxation time was kept down to a value of less than one second.

The results are shown in Fig. 15.2 on successively expanded temperature scales. We see that the specific heat continues to rise as we continue to approach the lambda temperature. Fig. 15.3 shows the same results for the specific heat at temperature T plotted against the logarithm of $|T-T_\lambda|$. The results above and below the lambda point fall respectively on lines which may be written empirically as

$$C_{\text{svp}} = -0\cdot65 - 3\cdot00\log_{10}|T-T_\lambda|, \qquad T > T_\lambda$$

$$C_{\text{svp}} = 4\cdot55 - 3\cdot00\log_{10}|T-T_\lambda|, \qquad T < T_\lambda.$$

That is, the specific heat goes logarithmically to infinity as we approach the lambda line. (Note that the specific heat of a finite sample will never reach infinity, as thermal fluctuations set a lower limit to observable values of $|T-T_\lambda|$.) This logarithmic anomaly is reflected in many of the other thermodynamic properties. Thus Fig. 15.4 shows values of the coefficient $(\partial P/\partial T)_v$ measured along a line of constant volume; the

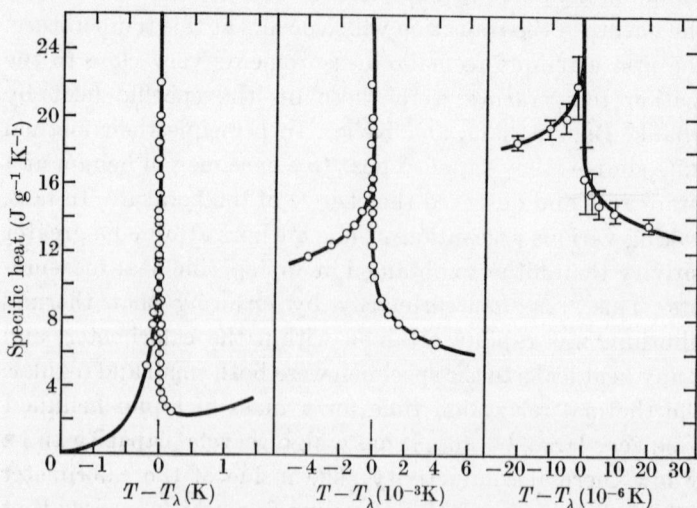

FIG. 15.2. The specific heat of liquid ⁴He under the saturated vapour pressure as a function of $T-T_\lambda$. The width of the small vertical line just above the origin indicates the portion of the diagram shown expanded (in width) in the curve directly to the right (after Buckingham and Fairbank [98]).

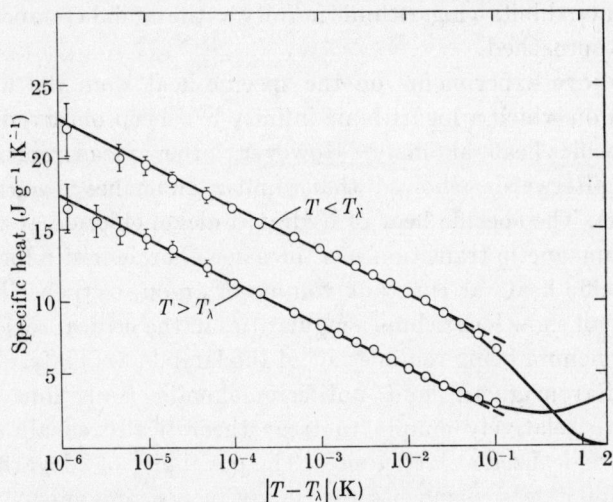

FIG. 15.3. The specific heat of liquid ^{4}He under the saturated vapour pressure plotted against $|T-T_\lambda|$ (after Buckingham and Fairbank [98]).

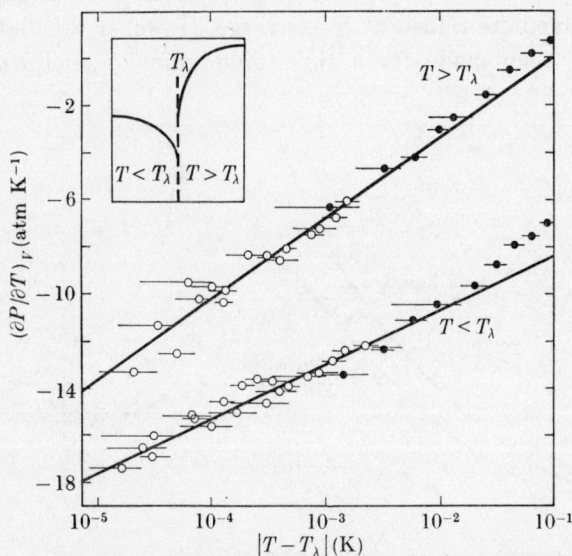

FIG. 15.4. Values of $(\partial P/\partial T)_V$ measured along the isochore $V = V_\lambda (P \simeq 13$ atm, $T_\lambda = 2\cdot023$ K). The black circles are due to Lounasmaa and Kaunisto [99]. The horizontal lines on each point show the temperature increment used in determining $(\partial P/\partial T)_V$ (Lounasmaa [100]).

coefficient exhibits a logarithmic infinity as the lambda temperature is approached.

The above experiments on the specific heat were the first
occasion on which a logarithmic infinity had been observed in
any specific heat anomaly. However, other measurements
shortly afterwards, showed that similar anomalies occurred
elsewhere. The specific heat of hydrated nickel chloride at the
antiferromagnetic transition has the same characteristic form.
The specific heats at constant volume of argon, oxygen, ^{3}He,
and ^{4}He all show logarithmic singularities in the critical region,
those in helium being reminiscent of the lambda anomaly.

The ferromagnetic and antiferromagnetic transitions in
solids are relatively simple to treat theoretically as all the
atoms are localized at lattice sites. The possibility of a logarithmic infinity was demonstrated many years previously by
Onsager for the hypothetical case of a simple model with a
two-dimensional lattice. A generalization of this result to three
dimensions is difficult because the terms in the various expan-
sions involved are reluctant to converge. However calculations
have now been made for a three-dimensional model with a

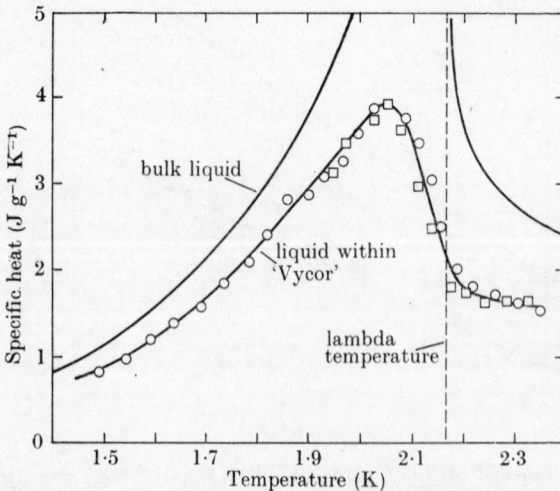

FIG. 15.5. The specific heat of liquid ^{4}He contained with the pores of 'Vycor'
porous glass (Brewer, Champeney, and Mendelssohn [103]).

diamond-type lattice, which also leads to a logarithmic infinity. For a general discussion of this work see references [101, 102].

Finally, we note that the lambda point is shifted to lower temperatures if the liquid helium is confined within very narrow channels. The effect of channel size has been studied by measuring the specific heat of liquid helium confined in the channels of 'Vycor' porous glass, which have diameters of the order of 50 Å. Figure 15.5 shows both a shift of the transition to lower temperatures and a smoothing of the specific heat anomaly.

Although the lambda transition is clearly the analogue in liquid ^{4}He of the Bose condensation in a perfect gas, the analogy is not at all a close one. The specific heat of a perfect gas shows no logarithmic infinity, and below the transition varies with temperature as $T^{3/2}$, much less rapidly than in helium II. The lambda transition shifts to lower temperatures when the liquid is compressed, whereas the opposite effect is expected in a perfect gas. Similarly the observed scattering of light and neutrons by helium at the transition is predicted incorrectly by the gas model. There is as yet no complete account of the lambda transition in liquid helium, and further work is necessary; for an account of some current discussions see reference [104].

REFERENCES

1. LONDON, F., *Superfluids*, Vol. 2 (Wiley 1954).
2. SWENSON, C. A., *Phys. Rev.* **79**, 626 (1950).
3. ATKINS, K. R., *Liquid Helium* (Cambridge University Press, 1959).
4. ABEL, W. R., ANDERSON, A. C., BLACK, W. C., and WHEATLEY, J. C., *Physics* **1**, 337 (1965).
5. ABRAHAM, B. M., OSBORNE, D. W., and WEINSTOCK, B., *Phys. Rev.* **98**, 551 (1955).
6. ROBERTS, T. R. and SYDORIAK, S. G., *Phys. Rev.* **98**, 1672 (1955).
7. BREWER, D. F., DAUNT, J. G., and SREEDHAR, A. K., *Phys. Rev.* **115**, 836 (1959).
8. THOMSON, A. L., MEYER, H., and ADAMS, E. D., *Phys. Rev.* **128**, 509 (1962).
9. BETTS, D. S., OSBORNE, D. W., WELBER, B., and WILKS, J., *Phil. Mag.* **8**, 977 (1963).
10. BETTS, D. S., KEEN, B. E., and WILKS, J., *Proc. R. Soc.* **A289**, 34 (1965).
11. LEE, D. M. and FAIRBANK, H. A., *Phys. Rev.* **116**, 1359 (1959).
12. ANDERSON, A. C., SALINGER, G. L., and WHEATLEY, J. C., *Phys. Rev. Lett.* **6**, 443 (1961).
13. LANDAU, L. D., *Soviet Phys. JETP* **3**, 920 (1957).
14. BROOKER, G. A. and SYKES, J., *Phys. Rev. Lett.* **21**, 279 (1968).
15. DY, K. S. and PETHICK, C. J., *Phys., Rev. Lett.* **21**, 876 (1968).
16. LANDAU, L. D., *Soviet Phys. JETP* **5**, 101 (1957).
17. ABEL, W. R., ANDERSON, A. C., and WHEATLEY, J. C., *Phys. Rev. Lett.* **17**, 74 (1966).
18. KIRBY, I. J. and WILKS, J., *J. Phys. C (Proc. phys. Soc.)* **1**, 555 (1968).
19. WHEATLEY, J. C., *Phys. Rev.* **165**, 304 (1968).
20. DONIACH, S., *Proc. 11th Int. Conf. Low Temp. Phys.*, eds. ALLEN, FINLAYSON, and McCOLL (University of St. Andrews, 1968), Vol. 1, p. 76.
21. KUPER, C. G., *An Introduction to the Theory of Superconductivity* (Clarendon Press, 1968).
22. ANDERSON, A. C., ROACH, W. R., SARWINSKI, R. E., and WHEATLEY, J. C., *Phys. Rev. Lett.* **16**, 263 (1966).
23. EDWARDS, D. O., *Proc. 11th Int. Conf. Low Temp. Phys.*, eds. ALLEN, FINLAYSON, and McCOLL (University of St. Andrews, 1968), Vol. 1, p. 352.
24. EDWARDS, D. O., BAUM, J. L., BREWER, D. F., DAUNT, J. G., and McWILLIAMS, A. S., *Proc. 7th Int. Conf. Low Temp. Phys.*, eds. GRAHAM and HOLLIS-HALLETT (North-Holland, 1961) p. 610.

25. LE PAIR, C., TACONIS, K. W., DE BRUYN OUBOTER, R., and DAS, P. *Physica, 's Grav.* **29**, 755 (1963).
26. HOLLIS-HALLETT, A. C., *Prog. Low Temp. Phys.*, ed. GORTER (North-Holland, 1955), Vol. 1, p. 64.
27. DAUNT, J. G., and MENDELSSOHN, K., *Proc. R. Soc.* **A170**, 423 (1939).
28. KEESOM, W. H., SARIS, B. F., and MEYER, L., *Physica, 's Grav.* **7**, 817 (1940).
29. WINKEL, P., BROESE VON GROENOU, A., and GORTER, C. J., *Physica, 's Grav.* **21**, 345 (1955).
30. BREWER, D. F. and EDWARDS, D. O., *Phil. Mag.* **6**, 775 (1961).
31. PESHKOV, V. P., *J. Phys. Moscow* **10**, 389 (1946); *Soviet Phys. J.E.T.P.* **11**, 580 (1960).
32. HALL, H. E., *Proc. phys. Soc.* **A67**, 485 (1954).
33. LANDAU, L. D., *J. Phys. Moscow* **5**, 71 (1941); **11**, 91 (1947).
34. LIFSHITZ, E. M. and ANDRONIKASHVILI, E. L., *A Supplement to Helium* (Consultants Bureau Inc., 1959).
35. PELLAM, J. R. and HANSON, W. B., *Phys. Rev.* **85**, 216 (1952).
36. STEDMAN, R., ALMQUIST, L., NILSSON, G., and RAUNIO, G., *Phys. Rev.* **162**, 545 (1967).
37. WILKS, J., *The Third Law of Thermodynamics* (Oxford University Press, 1961) p. 77.
38. FAIRBANK, H. A. and WILKS, J., *Proc. R. Soc.* **A231**, 545 (1955).
39. COHEN, M. and FEYNMAN, R. P., *Phys. Rev.* **107**, 13 (1957).
40. HENSHAW, D. G. and WOODS, A. D. B., *Phys. Rev.* **121**, 1266 (1961).
41. BENDT, P. J., COWAN, R. D., and YARNELL, J. L., *Phys. Rev.* **113**, 1386 (1959).
42. KRAMERS, H. C., *Proc. K. ned. Akad. Wet.* **B59**, 35 and 48 (1956).
43. ACKERMAN, C. C. and GUYER, R. A., *Ann. Phys.* **50**, 128 (1968).
44. KHALATNIKOV, I. M., *Usp. fiz. Nauk.* **59**, 673 (1956).
45. ZINOV'EVA, K. N., *Soviet Phys. JETP* **4**, 36 (1957).
46. HANSON, W. B. and PELLAM, J. R., *Phys. Rev.* **95**, 321 (1954).
47. ATKINS, K. R. and HART, K. H., *Phys. Rev.* **92**, 204 (1953).
48. KHALATNIKOV, I. M., *Usp. fiz. Nauk.* **60**, 69 (1956).
49. DRANSFELD, K., NEWELL, J. A., and WILKS, J., *Proc. R. Soc.* **A243**, 500 (1958).
50. KHALATNIKOV, I. M. and CHERNIKOVA, D. M., *Soviet Phys. JETP* **23**, 274 (1966).
51. CHALLIS, L. J., DRANSFELD, K., and WILKS, J., *Proc. R. Soc.* **A260**, 31 (1961).
52. FAIRBANK, H. A. and WILKS, J., *Proc. R. Soc.* **A231**, 545 (1955).
53. ABEL, W. R., ANDERSON, A. C., BLACK, W. C., and WHEATLEY, J. C., *Phys. Rev. Lett.* **16**, 273 (1966).
54. CHALLIS, L. J. and CHEEKE, J. D. N., *Proc. R. Soc.* **A304**, 479 (1968).
55. CHALLIS, L. J., *Phys. Lett.* **26A**, 105 (1968).
56. TACONIS, K. W. and DE BRUYN OUBOTER, R., *Prog. Low Temp. Phys.*, ed. GORTER (North-Holland, 1964), **4**, 38.

57. DE BRUYN OUBOTER, R., TACONIS, K. W., LE PAIR, C., and BEENAKKER, J. J. M., *Physica, 's Grav.* **26**, 853 (1960).
58. PELLAM, J. R., *Phys. Rev.* **99**, 1327 (1955).
59. GUTTMAN, L. and ARNOLD, J. R., *Phys. Rev.* **92**, 547 (1953).
60. STAAS, F. A., TACONIS, K. W., and FOKKENS, K., *Physica, 's Grav.* **26**, 699 (1960).
61. HARDING, G. O. and WILKS, J., *Proc. R. Soc.* **A268**, 424 (1962).
62. KING, J. C. and FAIRBANK, H. A., *Phys. Rev.* **93**, 21 (1954).
63. REIF, F. and MEYER, L., *Phys. Rev.* **119**, 1164 (1960).
64. TACONIS, K. W., *Prog. Low Temp. Phys.* ed. GORTER (North-Holland, 1961), **3**, 153.
65. BETTS, D. S., *Contemp. Phys.* **9**, 97 (1968).
66. WHEATLEY, J. C., VILCHES, O. E., and ABEL, W. R., *Physics* **4**, 1 (1968).
67. LONDON, H. and MENDOZA, E., *Proc. 11th Int. Conf. Low Temp. Phys.*, ed. ALLEN, FINLAYSON, and McCOLL (University of St. Andrews, 1968), Vol. 1, p. 86.
68. VILCHES, O. E. and WHEATLEY, J. C., *Phys. Lett.* **24A**, 440 (1967).
69. FEYNMAN, R. P., *Phys. Rev.* **91**, 1301 (1953); **94**, 262 (1954).
70. FEYNMAN, R. P., *Prog. Low Temp. Phys.*, ed. GORTER (North-Holland, 1955), **1**, 17.
71. FEYNMAN, R. P. and COHEN, M., *Phys. Rev.* **102**, 1189 (1956).
72. OSBORNE, D. V., *Proc. phys. Soc.* **A63**, 909 (1950).
73. HALL, H. E., *Phil. Trans. R. Soc.* **A250**, 359 (1957).
74. HALL, H. E. and VINEN, W. F., *Proc. R. Soc.* **A238**, 204 (1956).
75. HALL, H. E., *Proc. R. Soc.* **A245**, 546 (1958).
76. LANDAU, L. D. and LIFSHITZ, E. M., *Statistical Physics* (Pergamon Press, 1958), p. 103.
77. VINEN, W. F., *Proc. R. Soc.* **A260**, 218 (1961).
78. HALL, H. E., *Phil. Trans. R. Soc.* **A250**, 368 (1957).
79. HESS, G. B. and FAIRBANK, W. M., *Phys. Rev. Lett.* **19**, 216 (1967).
80. RAYFIELD, G. W. and REIF, F., *Phys. Rev. Lett.* **11**, 305 (1963); *Phys. Rev.* **136**, A1194 (1964).
81. REPPY, J. D. and DEPATIE, D., *Phys. Rev. Lett.* **12**, 187 (1964).
82. CLOW, J., WEAVER, J. C., DEPATIE, D., and REPPY, J. D., *Low Temperature Physics* L.T. 9., ed. DAUNT et al. (Plenum Press, 1965), p. 328.
83. MEHL, J. B. and ZIMMERMANN, W., *Phys. Rev. Lett.* **14**, 815 (1965); *Phys. Rev.* **167**, 214 (1968).
84. HALL, H. E., *Phil. Mag. Suppl.* **9**, 89 (1960).
85. VINEN, W. F., *Proc. R. Soc.* **A240**, 114 (1957).
86. MEYER, L. and REIF, F., *Phys. Rev.* **123**, 727 (1961).
87. PESHKOV, V. P. and STRYUKOV, V. B., *Soviet Phys. JETP* **14**, 1031 (1962).
88. DONNELLY, R. J. and HOLLIS HALLETT, A. C., *Ann. Phys.* **3**, 320 (1958).
89. DE BRUYN OUBOTER, R., TACONIS, K. W., and VAN ALPHEN, W. M., *Prog. Low Temp. Phys.*, ed. GORTER (North-Holland, 1967) **5**, 44.
90. LIN, C. C., *Liquid Helium*, ed. CARERI (Academic Press, 1963), p. 93.

91. VINEN, W. F., *Liquid Helium*, ed. CARERI (Academic Press, 1963), p. 336.
92. GLABERSON, W. I. and DONNELLY, R. J., *Phys. Rev.* **141,** 208 (1966).
93. BRUSCHI, L., MAZZOLDI, P., and SANTINI, M., *Phys. Rev.* **167,** 203 (1968).
94. BOGOLIUBOV, N. N., *J. Phys. Moscow* **11,** 23 (1947).
95. RICHARDS, P. L. and ANDERSON, P. W., *Phys. Rev. Lett.* **14,** 540 (1965).
96. KHORANA, B. M. and CHANDRASEKHAR, B. S., *Phys. Rev. Lett.* **18,** 230 (1967).
97. ANDERSON, P. W., *Quantum Fluids*, ed. BREWER (North-Holland, 1966) p. 146.
98. BUCKINGHAM, M. J. and FAIRBANK, W. M., *Prog. Low Temp. Phys.*, ed. GORTER (North-Holland, 1961) **3,** 80.
99. LOUNASMAA, O. and KAUNISTO, L., *Ann. Acad. Sci. Fenn. Sev. AVI (Finland)* No. 59 (1960).
100. LOUNASMAA, O. V., *Phys. Rev.* **130,** 847 (1963).
101. BROUT, R., *Low Temperature Physics*, L.T.9, ed. DAUNT *et al.* (Plenum Press, 1965), Part B, p. 623.
102. DOMB, C., *Low Temperature Physics* L.T.9, ed. DAUNT *et al.* (Plenum Press, 1965), Part B, p. 637.
103. BREWER, D. F., CHAMPENEY, D. C., and MENDELSSOHN, K., *Cryogenics* **1,** 108 (1960).
104. ALLEN, FINLAYSON, and McCOLL (editors) *Proc. 11th Int. Conf. Low Temp. Phys.* (University of St. Andrews, 1968), Vol. 1, pp. 27, 195–220, 323.

INDEX

Kapitza resistance, 88
kinetic coefficients, 80 ff.

lambda transition, 5, 36, 153 ff.
lifetime of states, 17, 62
linear region defined, 41

magnetic susceptibility of
Fermi gas, 12
^{3}He, 8, 21
solutions, 32
melting curve, 3
^{3}He, 33
^{4}He, 3, 35
melting, heat of, 5
mixing, heat of, 102
molar volume, 2
momentum of
heat flow, 43, 54
normal fluid, 73, 75
phonons, 63
mutual friction, 132

neutrons, scattering of, 61
normal fluid
density, 45, 49, 50, 72
^{3}He atoms, 93, 95
viscosity, 50, 81
Normal processes, 59, 79

osmotic pressure of solutions, 94

paramagnons, 29
persistent currents, 127
perturbation theory of ^{3}He, 27
phase separation, 91
phase slip, 151
phonons
in helium, 59, 104, 150
momentum of, 63
in solids, 57

quasi-particles, 16, 27
see excitations

Rayleigh disc, 55
relaxation processes, 87

rotating helium, 115 ff.
angular momentum, 118, 130
heat flow in, 120
second sound in, 119
two-fluid model, 119
vortices, 122
rotons, 65, 113

second sound, 42, 77
absorption of, 84, 132
in rotating helium, 119, 132
in solids, 80
and turbulence, 135
velocity of, 48
second viscosity, 87
solutions of ^{3}He in helium II, 31, 91
osmotic pressure of, 94
sound, absorption in
^{3}He, 24
^{4}He, 85
solutions, 98
sound, velocity in ^{3}He, 13, 21
specific heat
Fermi gas, 11
^{3}He, 7, 21, 28
^{4}He, 5, 59, 64
near lambda point, 153
solutions, 32, 92
superfluid,
density of, 45
persistent currents, 127
wave functions of, 114
superfluidity, 5, 36
and Bose condensation, 151
possibility of in ^{3}He, 29
theory of, 68
symmetry of wave function, 20, 106, 126

temperature waves, see second sound
thermal boundary resistance, 88
thermal conductivity
Fermi gas, 14
^{3}He, 10, 22, 28
solids, 58
see heat flow in helium II

thermal kinetic coefficient K, 83
thermomechanical effect, 38, 52
Third Law of Thermodynamics, 5,
    34, 92
turbulence, 42, 134, 139, 141
two-fluid model, 44 ff.
  equations of motion, 46
  in rotating helium, 119
  theoretical basis, 67 ff., 112

Umklapp processes, 59, 79
uncertainty principle, 17, 57

Van der Waals forces, 1
viscosity of
  Fermi gas, 13

^{3}He, 8, 22
^{4}He, 36
normal fluid, 50, 81
solutions, 97
vortex lines, 122 ff
  and excitations, 130
  oscillation of, 133
vortex rings, 129, 145
  and phase slip, 152

wave functions of
  helium II, 103 ff.
  solute atoms, 111

zero-point energy, 1
zero sound, 23